ONLINE PASSIVE INCOME BUSINESS

I0698526

VONETTE NIXON

A Strategy for Accelerating Your Online Business's Financial Success

Table of Contents

Introduction

The appeal of online passive income enterprises has captivated the imagination of innumerable individuals seeking financial freedom, flexibility, and autonomy in the ever-changing landscape of modern entrepreneurship. We live in an era where the internet has broken down traditional entry barriers, allowing anyone with an internet connection and a spark of imagination to embark on a road toward economic independence.

This eBook, "Online Passive Income Business: A Strategy for Accelerating Your Online Business's Financial Success," provides a guide through the complex web of options that the digital world offers. Whether you're a seasoned entrepreneur trying to diversify your income streams or a beginner beginning from scratch, this comprehensive guide will provide you with the knowledge, tools, and tactics you need to turn your online business into a source of passive income.

Imagine a life where your financial future isn't solely determined by the number of hours you put in each day but by the systems you've put in place, humming away in the background, creating cash while you sleep, travel, or follow your interests. That is the promise of passive income, and this eBook is your guide to realizing it.

We'll look at the fundamentals of passive income, dive into different online business ideas, and learn how to create high-quality content that resonates with your audience. You'll learn about monetization tactics that can transform your passion into profit, as well as how to automate your business operations, freeing up your time to focus on what really matters to you.

As we progress through the pages of this eBook, we'll examine the complexities of digital marketing and promotion, the need to scale your firm for long-term success, and important financial and tax issues. Along the way, you'll discover essential lessons from real-life success stories and how to avoid common errors that can stymie your progress.

So, whether you want to augment your current income, escape the 9-to-5 grind, or attain ultimate financial freedom, your journey begins here. Welcome to the world of online passive income enterprises, where you can accelerate your financial success and embrace a life of plenty, creativity, and fulfillment with the correct methods and unrelenting drive.

Chapter 1: Understanding the Power of Passive Income

In the grand scope of financial goals, one concept stands out as a game changer: passive income. It's the secret sauce that enables people to break free from the constraints of standard 9-to-5 work and embark on a path to financial freedom and flexibility. But what precisely is passive income, and why is it so appealing?

Passive income is defined as earnings that do not necessitate active, day-to-day involvement. It is the money you earn while sleeping, traveling, spending time with loved ones, or pursuing your passions. Imagine waking up to find your bank account a little fatter than it was the day before, all without you lifting a finger. That is the allure of passive income.

The allure of passive income is its ability to divorce your time from your profits. In traditional employment, your pay is proportionate to the number of hours you work. You are not paid if you do not work. However, when you have passive income, the assets, investments, or processes you've put in place are what generate the money, and they continue to do so whether or not you're actively working.

Consider real estate investing. When you own rental properties, the rent payments you get each month can be a source of passive income. Dividends from investments, royalties from a book or music CD, and affiliate marketing commissions are all examples of passive income.

The benefits of passive income go beyond monetary gain. It allows you to live your life on your own terms. Want to tour the world, spend more time with your family, or follow a lifetime passion? Passive income can help make these ambitions a reality.

However, it is critical to understand that passive income is not a miraculous answer to rapid prosperity. It necessitates hard work, devotion, and, in many cases, a significant initial investment of time, money, or both. In the next chapters, we'll look at various strategies and approaches for maximizing the potential of passive income and creating an internet business that can generate cash on autopilot.

So, as we dig deeper into the world of online passive income businesses, keep in mind the transforming power of passive income. It's not just about generating money; it's about reclaiming your time, obtaining financial security, and establishing a life that corresponds with your goals and values. Are you ready to open the door to financial independence? Let us begin our trip together.

The Idea of Passive Income

Passive income is a concept that has captured the imaginations of countless people looking for financial independence and a better quality of life. It deviates from the usual concept of exchanging time for money, in which your salary is directly proportional to the number of hours you labor. Instead, passive income enables you to create money streams that continue to flow even when you are not actively working. It's like having money work for you rather than against you.

Passive income, at its heart, is the product of wise investments, methods, or assets. These investments provide profits with little to no continuous work on your side. The allure of passive income stems from its capacity to provide financial stability, security, and the flexibility to live life on your own terms.

There are several types of passive income, each with its own distinct characteristics:

1. **Rental Income:** Owning and renting out real estate, whether residential or commercial, can provide a consistent stream of passive income. Rent payments from tenants contribute to your income without your ongoing engagement.
2. **Dividend Stocks**: Investing in dividend-paying stocks allows you to consistently receive a piece of a company's income. These dividends are normally paid out regularly, providing a consistent source of income.
3. **Savings or bond interest:** Savings accounts, certificates of deposit (CDs), and bonds all pay interest over time. While the rewards are modest, they take very little work on your behalf.
4. **Royalties:** When your intellectual property, such as books, music, or artwork, is used or sold, you might receive royalties. This can generate revenue long after you've published the material.
5. **Affiliate Marketing:** Using affiliate programs to promote products or services allows you to earn commissions on purchases produced by your recommendations. It is a popular choice among online entrepreneurs.

Building and developing online companies, such as e-commerce stores, blogs, or YouTube channels, can generate passive revenue via advertising, affiliate marketing, or product sales.

While passive income provides tremendous prospects, it is critical to remove the myth that it requires no initial work. In practice, creating and maintaining these income streams frequently takes significant upfront work, attention, and, in some cases, financial investment. Furthermore, passive income is not completely hands-off; some amount of management and maintenance may be required.

In the following chapters, we'll look at ways to create passive income through online enterprises, giving you the information and skills, you need to create a long-term source of income. You may take big strides toward financial independence and living the life you want by understanding the concept of passive income and leveraging its potential.

Passive Income Benefits and Drawbacks

With all of its attractiveness and promise for financial freedom, passive income has its fair share of benefits and drawbacks. Before beginning your quest to generate passive income streams, it's critical to grasp both sides of the coin in order to make informed decisions and set realistic expectations.

The Benefits of Passive Income:

1. **Financial Independence:** The most major benefit of passive income is that it can release you from the constraints of a typical 9-to-5 job. It gives you financial security and the freedom to live your life on your own terms.
2. Passive income enables you to regain your time. You are no longer restricted to exchanging hours for bucks, allowing you to pursue other interests, travel, or spend time with loved ones.
3. **Diversification:** Creating various passive income streams can help you diversify your revenue sources and reduce your reliance on a single job or business.
4. **Growth Potential:** With perseverance and effective techniques, passive income streams can develop over time, potentially surpassing your active income.
5. **Asset Creation:** Many passive income sources, such as rental properties or online enterprises, can result in the creation of valuable assets that can increase in value over time.
6. **Tax Advantages:** Some passive income sources provide tax benefits, such as deductions and lower tax rates for specific investments.

Passive Income Drawbacks:

1. **Initial Effort:** Creating passive income streams frequently takes a large amount of initial effort, which includes research, investment, and continuous maintenance.
2. **Uncertainty and Risk:** Not all passive income ventures are guaranteed to succeed, and there is always some risk involved. Market or economic factors may have an impact on income.
3. **Longer-Term Perspective:** Generating significant passive income takes time. You might not see quick benefits, so be patient.

4. While passive income requires less engagement on a daily basis, it still necessitates periodic inspection and maintenance to guarantee that your revenue streams remain viable.
5. **Market Volatility:** Some forms of passive income, such as stocks, are susceptible to market volatility. This means that your earnings may vary depending on market conditions.
6. **Initial Capital:** Many passive income possibilities, such as real estate or investments, may necessitate a substantial initial capital investment, which may not be available to everyone.
7. Understanding the nuances of various passive income strategies can be difficult, and a high learning curve may be required.

Finally, while passive income can be a valuable tool for obtaining financial independence and flexibility, it is not a one-size-fits-all answer. It has its own set of benefits and drawbacks that must be properly considered. Your passive income options should be chosen in accordance with your financial objectives, risk tolerance, and available resources. While there may be obstacles to overcome, the potential advantages of earning passive income will be well worth the time and effort you put into your quest.

Different passive income streams

Passive income does not come in one size fits all. There are numerous paths you can take to generate passive income streams, each with its own set of features and prospects. Understanding these many possibilities can help you choose the course that best suits your interests, resources, and financial objectives.

Consider the following common passive revenue streams:

1. **Rental Properties:** Owning and renting out real estate is a classic example of passive income. Rental income can provide a consistent cash flow, but it does necessitate initial investments, property management, and periodic maintenance.
2. **Dividend Stocks:** Investing in dividend-paying stocks allows you to share in the profitability of a firm. Dividends are usually paid out on a regular basis, providing a source of passive income. Remember that stock investments are risky.
3. **Savings and bond interest:** Money maintained in savings accounts, certificates of deposit (CDs), or bonds can earn interest income. While the returns may be modest, the risks are quite minimal.
4. **Royalties:** If you create intellectual property such as books, music, patents, or artwork, you might receive royalties when others use or buy it. This can provide long-term passive income.
5. **Affiliate Marketing:** You can earn money on sales produced by your referral links by advertising products or services through affiliate networks. For online marketers and bloggers, this can be a lucrative alternative.
6. **Online Advertising:** If you have a successful blog, YouTube channel, or website, you can generate passive income through advertising. Google AdSense and affiliate advertising can help you monetize your content.
7. **E-commerce Stores:** By creating an e-commerce store and drop shipping products, you can earn money from online sales. While there is some labor required in setting up and marketing the store, with the correct procedures in place, it may become passive.
8. **Peer-to-Peer Lending:** Through platforms such as Prosper and Lending Club, you can lend money to people or small businesses in exchange for interest payments. It's a type of passive income with considerable risk.

9. **Create Online Courses or eBooks:** Passive income can be generated by sharing your expertise by creating and selling online courses or eBooks. They can be sold repeatedly after they have been produced.
10. **Subscription Services:** Creating a subscription-based business, such as a membership site or a software-as-a-service (SaaS) platform, can provide subscribers with regular monthly income.
11. **Crowdfunding for Real Estate:** Instead of purchasing full properties, you can invest in real estate using crowdfunding platforms. These investments can generate rental income as well as capital appreciation.
12. **License Your Photography or Artwork:** If you're a photographer or artist, you can earn royalties by licensing your work for use in advertisements, periodicals, or goods.
13. **Automated Drop shipping:** Using automated drop shipping in your online store allows you to sell products without having to manage inventory or shipment, making it a possible source of passive revenue.
14. **Peer-to-Peer Car Rental:** If you own a vehicle, platforms such as Turo allow you to rent it to others when you aren't using it, making rental income.
15. **Develop a Mobile App:** Creating a mobile app and monetizing it with ads or in-app purchases might generate passive revenue if it becomes popular.

Keep in mind that the level of passive involvement varies between various income streams. Some may necessitate a greater initial investment or continuing care than others. Diversifying your passive income streams might also provide better stability and protection from market changes. Consider your hobbies, talents, resources, and risk tolerance when choosing passive income streams to identify the best fit for your financial goals.

Chapter 2: Identifying Niche and Target Audience

Identifying your specialty and understanding your target audience is a critical step in developing a successful online passive income business. This approach lays the groundwork for the rest of your enterprise, creating your content, goods, and marketing methods. Here's a closer look at why it's important and how to get started:

Why is it significant?

1. **Focus and Direction:** Defining your specialization helps you focus your efforts by narrowing your range of competence. It's all about identifying your distinct angle or area of competence within a larger business or market.
2. **Audience Connection:** Knowing your target audience enables you to speak directly to their wants, preferences, and problem points. This relationship generates trust and a loyal following.
3. **Competitive Advantage:** A well-defined niche can set you apart from competitors, making it simpler to stand out in a congested online arena.
4. **Relevance of Content:** The sort of content you develop is dictated by your niche and target audience, ensuring that it is valuable and resonates with them.

How to Find Your Niche:

1. **Create Buyer Personas:** Begin by thinking about your personal passions, hobbies, and interests. What topics or hobbies actually interest you? Building a business around your passion may be extremely rewarding.
2. **competence:** Evaluate your abilities, knowledge, and competence. What are you particularly talented at? Your knowledge and experience might be a useful advantage in your chosen field.
3. **Market Research:** Conduct extensive market research to uncover industry trends and gaps. Look for ways to add value or offer solutions.
4. **Solve Their Problems:** Pay attention to what people are actively searching for on the internet. Popular topics and queries can be identified using keyword research tools and forums.

5. **Analysis of Competitors:** Research your intended niche's competitors. Examine their strengths and flaws, and search for places where you may stand out.

Understanding Your Target Audience:

1. **Create Buyer Personas:** Detailed profiles of your ideal buyers should be created. Include demographics, interests, pain spots, and objectives. This enables you to personalize your content and goods to their individual requirements.
2. **Engage Your Audience:** Use social media, forums, or surveys to interact with your target audience. Inquire about their concerns and solicit opinions.
3. **Analyze Analytics:** Gather data on your audience's behavior by using website and social media analytics. Keep track of the material they interact with the most and change your strategy accordingly.
4. **Solve Their Issues:** Determine the issues and obstacles that your target audience confronts in your niche. Create content and products that address these pain spots and provide answers.
5. **Stay current:** Stay current on developments in your niche and growing trends among your target audience. Adapt your techniques to stay current and suit their changing needs.

Remember that establishing your niche and target audience is an ongoing activity, not a one-time task. You may fine-tune your approach and personalize your offerings as you learn more about your audience and specialty. Finally, a well-defined specialty and a thorough grasp of your target audience are the foundations of a profitable online passive income business. They direct your content creation, product development, and marketing efforts, ensuring that your company resonates with and serves the needs of your target audience.

Discovering your expertise and passion

One of the most important aspects of developing a successful online passive income business is capitalizing on your passion and experience. Your passion fuels your devotion, while your expertise serves as the foundation for establishing authority and credibility in your chosen field. Here's why identifying and harnessing these elements is critical:

Passion:

1. **Sustainable Motivation:** When you are enthusiastic about a topic or industry, you are more likely to stay motivated and committed to your business, even when faced with problems or losses.
2. **Enjoyment:** Building an online business requires time and effort, but if you enjoy what you're doing, it won't feel like a chore. Instead, it becomes a pleasurable activity.
3. **Authenticity:** Your work reflects your passion. It's seen in your content, goods, and interactions with your customers, making your company more genuine and relatable.
4. **Resilience:** People who are passionate about something are frequently more resilient. They are willing to learn from mistakes and keep going because they believe in what they are doing.

Expertise:

1. **Credibility:** Expertise in your sector or industry establishes your credibility and authority. People are more likely to trust and follow someone who is knowledgeable in their field.
2. **Quality material:** Because of your experience, you can generate high-quality, valuable material that actually benefits your audience. As a result, followers are attracted and retained.
3. **Problem Solving:** Your expertise enables you to recognize and solve difficulties in your field. This establishes you as a problem solver, which may result in higher demand for your products or services.
4. **Innovation:** When you are informed about your sector, you may innovate and bring new ideas and perspectives to your industry, distinguishing yourself from the competition.

How to Discover Your Passion:

1. **Self-reflection:** Consider what actually thrills and energizes you. Consider your hobbies, interests, and the things that naturally pique your attention.
2. **Experiment:** Don't be frightened to try anything new. Experiment with different niches or themes until you find one that speaks to you deeply.
3. **Seek Inspiration:** To obtain inspiration and identify possible passions, read books, watch videos, and follow thought leaders in many industries.
4. **Connect with Others:** Make contact with others who share your interests. Join forums, social media groups, or attend events connected to your possible passion to learn more and interact with other people who share your interests.

How to Use Your Expertise:

1. **Continuous Learning:** Maintain your commitment to learning and remaining current in your field. Taking courses, attending seminars, or reading business magazines can all help.
2. **Share Your Expertise:** Begin by sharing your knowledge through blogs, videos, podcasts, or social media. Providing useful knowledge is an excellent method to establish authority.
3. **Teach and Mentor:** Teach and mentor others by delivering workshops, webinars, or coaching services to share your knowledge and establish your expertise.
4. **Collaborate:** Work with other professionals in your field. Joint ventures and collaborations can boost your credibility and reach.

Remember that discovering your passion and honing your skills is a journey, not a destination. It may take some time and effort to discover what actually speaks to you. Once you've found your passion and polished your knowledge, you can leverage these assets to create an online passive income business that not only matches your interests but also resonates with your target audience, increasing your chances of success.

Market research and competitor analysis

When considering starting an online passive income business, two crucial tasks must not be overlooked: market research and competitor analysis. These techniques give you significant insights into your target audience and aid in your understanding of the competitive landscape in your selected sector. Here's why they're important and how to implement them:

Market Analysis:

1. **Identifying Opportunities:** Market research aids in the identification of opportunities within your selected sector. You'll identify market gaps, unmet demands, or rising trends that can be capitalized on for success.
2. **Understanding Your Audience:** Extensive research allows you to better grasp your target audience. You will learn about their preferences, pain areas, behaviors, and demographics.
3. **Tailoring Your Offerings:** With market research data at your disposal, you can design your products, services, and content to fit the precise expectations and aspirations of your target audience.
4. **Risk Reduction:** By completing thorough research, you lessen the risk of spending time and resources on a niche or business model that may not have enough demand or growth potential.

Market Research Methodology:

1. **Online Tools:** To identify popular search terms and subjects connected to your niche, use online tools such as Google Keyword Planner, SEMrush, or Ahrens.
2. **Surveys and Questionnaires:** Create surveys or questionnaires to collect information from your target audience directly. SurveyMonkey and Google Forms are two examples of useful tools.
3. **Competitor Analysis:** Analyze your competitors' websites, content, and customer reviews to learn more about their strengths and problems.
4. **Social Media Listening:** Monitoring social media channels and forums related to your niche to determine what themes and issues are currently trending.

Analysis of competitors:

1. **Identifying Competitors:** A competitive analysis will help you find your niche's direct and indirect competitors. This comprises both established and growing companies.
2. **Strengths and Weaknesses:** Examine the strengths and weaknesses of your competitors. This evaluation can help you plan your strategy by allowing you to capitalize on their flaws while avoiding their strengths.
3. **Market Positioning:** Market positioning is analyzing how your competitors position themselves in the market. Understanding their differentiating features (USPs) will help you differentiate your offers.
4. **Pricing tactics:** Research your competitors' pricing tactics to see where your items or services fit in terms of price and value.

How to Perform a Competitive Analysis:

1. **Online Research:** To find your competitors, undertake online research on search engines, social media, and industry-specific directories.
2. **Website Analysis:** Examine your competitors' websites for content, layout, user experience, and the items or services they provide.
3. **Customer Feedback:** Read customer reviews and testimonials to learn what customers like and dislike about your competitors' products.
4. **Benchmarking:** To identify opportunities for improvement, compare your business KPIs, such as pricing, customer service, and content quality, to those of your competitors.
5. **SWOT Analysis:** For each of your primary competitors, create a SWOT (Strengths, Weaknesses, Opportunities, Threats) analysis to illustrate their market position.

Market research and competitor analysis are constant procedures that continue long after your online passive income business has been launched. Staying up-to-date on changes in your area and keeping an eye on your competitors will help you alter your methods and stay competitive. While time-consuming, these processes are critical for creating a solid foundation for your firm and enhancing your prospects for long-term success.

Creating a Unique Selling Proposition

In the competitive world of online passive income businesses, having a unique selling proposition (USP) that distinguishes your brand and offerings from the competition is critical. Your USP is what distinguishes your company and makes it desirable and memorable to your target audience. Let's look at why a USP is vital and how to create one:

What Is the Importance of a Unique Selling Proposition?

1. **Differentiation:** In a congested market, a well-defined USP distinguishes you from the competition. It allows you to stand out and attract potential clients' attention.
2. **Value Proposition:** Your USP communicates the precise benefits and value your products or services provide to your target audience. It provides a solution to the question, "Why should I choose you?"
3. **Brand Identity:** A strong USP leads to the development of a distinct and memorable brand identity. It leaves a lasting impression in your customers' minds.
4. **Customer Attraction:** When your unique selling proposition (USP) resonates with your target demographic, it attracts the proper people who are more likely to become loyal, long-term customers.

How to Create a Standout Selling Proposition:

1. **Understand Your Audience:** Recognize the needs, pain areas, and preferences of your target audience. What issues are they attempting to address, and what solutions are they seeking? Your USP should correspond to their desires and ideals.
2. **Anal Your competition:** Research your competition to uncover market gaps and places where you can stand out. What do they provide, and how can you provide something better or different?
3. **Identify Your Strengths:** Consider your company's strengths, such as expertise, quality, pricing, customer service, or distinctive features. Determine what distinguishes you from others.
4. **Focus on Benefits:** Instead of describing features, stress the benefits your clients will receive by purchasing your products or services. How will their lives change?

5. **Create a clear message:** Your USP should be brief and easy to understand. In a sentence or two, it should explain your distinct worth. FedEx's USP, for example, is "when it absolutely, positively has to be there overnight."
6. **Test and refine:** Once you've created your USP, put it to the test with your target audience. Request feedback and, if necessary, make changes. Check to see if it resonates with your ideal clientele.

Unique selling proposition examples:

1. According to Domino's Pizza, "You get fresh, hot pizza delivered to your door in 30 minutes or less, or it's free."
2. "Think differently," says Apple.
3. "The world's largest selection," according to Amazon.
4. "M&M's," they say. "Melts in your mouth, not in your hand."
5. Nike says, "Just do it."
6. Lyft's slogan is "Rides in Minutes."
7. Shopify's motto is "Your business, your way."
8. MailChimp's motto is "Send better email."
9. Toms: "One for One."
10. Lululemon boasts of their products: "Sweat-wicking, four-way stretch, and engineered not to shrink."

Creating a compelling USP involves creativity, market awareness, and a strong connection with your target audience. It should capture the essence of your company and reflect your basic principles. Remember that a well-crafted USP is a continuing asset for your company, driving your marketing efforts and ensuring you remain a distinct and enticing option for your target clients.

Chapter 3: Choosing the Right Online Business Model

Your selected company model is the foundation of your success in the world of online passive income businesses. It determines how you earn income, the type of work necessary, and your ability to scale. This chapter goes into the essential process of choosing the best online business model, assisting you in making educated selections that are in accordance with your goals and resources.

Why the Right Business Model is Important:

1. **Alignment with Your Goals:** Your company model should be in line with your financial objectives, whether they be supplemental income, complete financial independence, or something in between.
2. **Using Your Strengths:** When selecting a company strategy, consider your abilities, expertise, and resources. Using your strengths to your advantage can provide you with a competitive advantage.
3. **Scalability:** Some business models scale better than others. Choose a plan that provides for scalability if you want to expand and improve your passive revenue over time.
4. **Resource and Time Commitment:** Different company strategies necessitate varying amounts of initial investment, continuous work, and time commitment. Determine how much you are willing and able to invest.

Common Passive Income Online Business Models:

1. **Affiliate Marketing:** Affiliate marketing allows you to promote products or services while earning commissions on sales produced by your referral links. Content generation and promotion are required.
2. **Drop shipping:** Drop shipping is the practice of opening an e-commerce store and selling things without keeping inventory. Product selection and promotion are required.
3. **Content Creation:** Create valuable information through blogs, YouTube channels, podcasts, and other formats. Advertise, sponsor, affiliate market, or sell your products to earn money.

4. **Membership Sites:** Create exclusive, subscription-based communities or content libraries that provide members with continuing value.
5. **Digital Products:** Develop and sell digital products such as e-books, online courses, templates, or software. It necessitates initial development but can be highly scalable.
6. **Print on Demand:** Create unique items such as T-shirts, mugs, or posters and have them created and distributed as customers place their orders. Inventory management is not necessary.
7. **Stock Photography or Art:** Allow agencies to use your photography or artwork in advertisements, publications, or merchandise.
8. **Subscription Boxes:** Subscribers receive new products on a regular basis.

Selecting the Best Model:

1. **Passion and Interest:** Select a model that corresponds to your passions and interests. It will make the work more fun and long-lasting.
2. **Market Demand:** Investigate market demand and competition for your preferred model. Is there a viable audience and potential for expansion?
3. **Initial Investment:** Determine your budget for launching and running your firm. Some models may necessitate a larger initial expenditure than others.
4. **Scalability:** Consider whether the approach permits you to increase your revenue as you grow. Can you improve your wages without raising your work proportionally?
5. **Availability of Resources:** Be realistic about the resources you have at your disposal, such as time, skills, and contacts. Select a model that complements your existing resources.
6. **Long-term viability:** Consider the model's long-term potential. Is it something you see yourself doing and benefiting from for the foreseeable future?
7. **Market Trends:** Keep up-to-date on market trends and new prospects within your selected model. Adapt your plan as necessary to stay competitive.

Remember that as you gain expertise and insights, the best business model for you may evolve. As your passive income business grows and changes, it's critical to remain adaptable and eager to pivot or diversify your income streams. Finally, choosing the right online company model is a critical step toward meeting your financial objectives and creating a thriving source of passive income.

Affiliate marketing

Affiliate marketing is a popular internet business concept that allows people to earn commissions by advertising other firms' products or services. Businesses benefit from increased exposure and revenue, while affiliate marketers' profit from their referrals. Let's take a look at how affiliate marketing works and how you can use it to generate passive revenue.

What is Affiliate Marketing?

1. **Join Affiliate Programs:** As an affiliate marketer, you begin by enrolling in affiliate programs provided by businesses or brands. These programs supply you with one-of-a-kind affiliate links or tracking codes.
2. **Select Products or Services:** Once you've joined an affiliate network, you can promote certain products or services. It is critical to select offerings that are relevant to your specialty and appealing to your target audience.
3. **Content Promotion:** You develop content to promote the selected items or services. Blog postings, product reviews, videos, social media posts, and email newsletters are all examples of content.
4. **Insert Affiliate Links:** You insert your affiliate links into your article. These links are unique to you and enable the company to track sales produced by your recommendations.
5. **Drive Traffic:** Your main goal is to get people to read your material. SEO (search engine optimization), social media marketing, email marketing, and other promotional tactics can help with this.
6. **receive Commissions:** You receive a commission or a percentage of the sale when your audience clicks on your affiliate links and makes a purchase or takes the required action (such as signing up for a service). Commissions might vary greatly based on the affiliate program and the price of the goods.

Affiliate Marketing Benefits:

1. **Low Entry Barrier:** Affiliate marketing involves little initial expenditure. You are not required to produce products, manage inventory, or give customer service.

2. **Scalability:** Affiliate marketing may be highly scalable with the appropriate tactics. You can promote a variety of products and broaden your reach.
3. **Diverse Niches:** Affiliate marketing opportunities are available in a variety of niches, making it accessible to people with diverse hobbies and industries.
4. After you've generated and marketed your material, it can continue to generate commissions even if you're not actively working on it.
5. You are not responsible for providing customer support, refunds, or product fulfillment. Your priority is to drive traffic and make recommendations.

Affiliate Marketing Difficulties:

1. The affiliate marketing field can be competitive, particularly for popular products or themes.
2. **Changing Algorithms:** Changes in search engine and social media algorithms can have an influence on your traffic and rankings, reducing your affiliate profits.
3. **Content Creation:** Creating high-quality content that converts on a consistent basis can be time-consuming and difficult.
4. **Income Variability:** Affiliate earnings can fluctuate due to factors such as seasonality, market trends, and your promotional activities.
5. Many affiliate programs require affiliates to declare their affiliate agreements, and noncompliance can result in penalties.

Affiliate Marketing Success Tips:

1. **Choosing High-Quality Products:** Promote products or services in which you have true faith and have tested. High-quality recommendations foster trust among your target audience.
2. **Create Valuable Content:** Focus on delivering value to your audience by creating content that is insightful, interesting, and well-researched.
3. Increase your online presence and audience by using SEO, social media, and email marketing. More commissions may result from a wider readership.
4. **Stay Informed:** To adjust your plan, keep up with industry developments, changes in affiliate programs, and digital marketing tactics.

5. **Diversify Income Sources:** To lessen reliance on a particular program or product, consider broadening your affiliate agreements.

Affiliate marketing can be a lucrative strategy to make online passive income. It enables you to earn commissions while assisting others in discovering useful items or services by using your experience and audience. While it may take some time to generate considerable income, affiliate marketing can become a reliable source of passive income with perseverance and smart marketing methods.

Drop shipping and e-commerce

Drop shipping and e-commerce are two internet business strategies that have grown in popularity in recent years. Both have the potential to generate passive income streams by selling things online, but they take different approaches and face different obstacles. Let's take a look at drop shipping and e-commerce and see how they function.

Drop shipping:

Drop shipping is a business concept in which you sell things to clients without maintaining any inventory. Rather, you collaborate with suppliers or wholesalers who manage product storage, packing, and shipping. Drop shipping operates as follows:

Choose a Niche: Select a niche or market area that fascinates you and has the potential for profit.

Locate reputable suppliers or wholesalers who provide drop shipping services in your chosen niche. Popular platforms include AliExpress and Salehi.

Set up an e-commerce website or use a platform such as Shopify, WooCommerce, or BigCommerce to develop your online store.

Import Products: Bring products from your preferred vendors into your business. These items are then put up for sale with your pricing.

Market Your Products: To attract potential buyers to your store, use digital marketing tactics such as SEO, social media marketing, email marketing, and paid advertising.

Order Processing: When a customer puts an order on your website, you send the order data to your supplier, who subsequently ships the product to the customer.

Profit: You make money by selling things at a higher price than the supplier charges you. Your margin is the difference between the selling price and the supplier's cost.

The Benefits of Drop shipping:

1. Drop shipping involves a low initial cost as compared to traditional retail operations.
2. There is no need to bother about warehousing, storage, or inventory management, which saves time and money.
3. **Scalability:** Adding more products or expanding into other niches is a reasonably simple way to scale your drop shipping business.
4. **Location Independence:** A drop shipping business may be conducted from anywhere with an internet connection, providing flexibility and freedom.

Drop shipping's Difficulties:

1. **smaller profit margins:** Because of increased competition and pricing constraints, drop shipping profit margins can be smaller than in traditional retail.
2. **Supplier Dependence:** The performance and dependability of your suppliers are critical to the success of your organization. A bad supplier can cause problems with customer service.
3. Drop shipping is a successful business model that has resulted in saturation and fierce rivalry in some categories.

E-commerce:

1. E-commerce, an abbreviation for electronic commerce, refers to the broader concept of selling goods or services over the internet. While drops hipping is a type of e-commerce, it also includes firms that handle their own inventory, warehousing, and order fulfillment. Here's how online shopping works:
2. **Select a Business Model:** Determine if you will sell your items, source them from manufacturers, or use a combination of the two.
3. Create an online store. Build an e-commerce website with platforms such as Shopify, Magento, WooCommerce, or custom development.
4. **Manage Inventory:** If you work with inventory, you must store, manage, and fulfill orders.
5. **Market and Promote:** To attract customers, use numerous marketing tactics such as SEO, content marketing, social media, and paid advertising.
6. **Order Fulfillment:** When customers place orders, you handle order fulfillment, which includes packaging and shipping.

7. Profits are earned by selling things at a markup above your costs, which include manufacturing, storage, and transportation.

Benefits of E-Commerce:

1. **bigger profit margins:** By procuring products at cheaper costs and setting competitive prices, e-commerce enterprises can possibly generate bigger profit margins.
2. **Inventory Management:** Inventory management gives you control over stock levels, quality, and fulfillment operations.
3. **Branding Possibilities:** E-commerce enables greater branding and product customization.

E-commerce's Difficulties:

1. **Inventory Costs:** There are costs associated with inventory management, such as storage, insurance, and the risk of overstocking or understocking.
2. **Logistics and Shipping:** Shipping logistics, particularly for international orders, can be complicated and costly.
3. **Consumer Service:** E-commerce companies are responsible for consumer queries, returns, and problem resolution.
4. E-commerce is a highly competitive industry that necessitates excellent marketing and differentiation methods.

Which is the best option for you?

Drop shipping has a lower barrier to entry and is great if you want to get started with a low initial cost. E-commerce gives you more control, but it also requires you to manage inventories and logistics. Some businesses use both approaches to diversify their revenue streams.

Finally, good marketing, offering value to customers, and constant improvement of your business processes are the keys to success in either drops hipping or e-commerce. When managed and scaled properly, both models have the ability to provide passive revenue.

Content creation and monetization

Content production is an effective way to share your knowledge, creativity, and skills with the rest of the world while simultaneously generating passive revenue. You can convert your hobby into a profitable internet business by providing valuable content and carefully monetizing it. Here's a guide to helping you understand content development and how to properly monetize it.

Making Content:

The process of generating and sharing useful, interesting, or helpful material with your intended audience is known as content development. This content can take many different forms, including:

1. **Blog posts:** written essays on specific areas of interest.
2. **Videos:** educational or entertaining videos that are shared on networks such as YouTube.
3. Podcasts are audio recordings that explore a variety of topics.
4. **E-books:** comprehensive guides or books on specialized themes.
5. Short-form content on sites such as Instagram, Twitter, and Facebook.
6. **Webinars:** These are live or recorded seminars on specific topics.
7. Visual representations of facts or information are known as infographics.
8. **Courses:** in-depth educational programs on certain topics.

Strategies for Monetization:

1. You may monetize valuable content in a variety of ways once you've developed it. Here are several popular approaches:
2. Display ads from platforms such as Google AdSense on your website or YouTube channel.
3. **Affiliate Marketing:** Use affiliate links to promote items or services within your content. Earn a commission on every sale made as a result of your referral.
4. **Sponsorships:** Collaborate with brands or businesses that are willing to pay you to promote their products or services in your content.

5. **Subscription Models:** For a regular price, provide your audience with premium material or exclusive access. Patrion and Sub stack are popular platforms for this strategy.
6. **Sell Digital Products:** Create and sell digital products relating to your niche, such as e-books, online courses, templates, or presets.
7. **products:** Create and sell branded products to your target demographic, such as T-shirts, mugs, or posters.
8. **Donations and Crowdfunding:** Allow your audience to support your work by making one-time donations (e.g., through PayPal) or by using crowdfunding sites such as Kickstarter or Indiegogo.
9. Create a membership-based community in which users pay for access to premium content, resources, or a community forum.

Best Content Creation and Monetization Practices:

1. **Understand Your Audience:** To develop content that resonates with your target audience, you must first understand their preferences, needs, and pain points.
2. Focus on producing high-quality, meaningful material rather than quantity. Delivering value on a consistent basis fosters trust and loyalty.
3. **SEO Optimization:** Learn and apply SEO tactics to increase the discoverability of your content on search engines.
4. **Diversify Income Streams:** Don't rely on a single method of monetization. To avoid risk, diversify your revenue sources.
5. **Transparency:** To preserve confidence with your audience, disclose any sponsored material or affiliate relationships.
6. Engage your audience. To develop a sense of community and loyalty, interact with your audience via comments, social media, or email.
7. **Stay Current:** To adapt and expand, stay current on industry developments, content creation tools, and monetization tactics.
8. **Patience and perseverance:** It take time to build a passive revenue stream through content development. Be patient and persistent, even if results are sluggish to appear.

Successful content creators include:

1. Neil Patel is a digital marketing specialist who shares excellent information via blog posts, videos, and podcasts. Profits from consulting services and training.

2. PewDiePie (Felix Kjellberg) is a YouTube content maker that specializes in gaming and entertainment. Advertisements, sponsorships, and products are used to generate revenue.
3. Many niche bloggers earn money by delivering in-depth information on certain topics, garnering a loyal readership, and monetizing through advertisements, affiliate marketing, and product sales.
4. Individuals such as Udemy instructors or developers on sites such as Teachable and Thingify sell courses on a variety of topics.
5. **Podcasters:** Sponsorships, premium material, and donations from dedicated listeners are common ways for podcasters to monetize.

Remember that while content creation might result in passive income, it usually necessitates a considerable upfront investment as well as ongoing content development. Building a dedicated following and diversifying your income streams are critical to achieving long-term passive income from content development.

Membership sites and subscription services

Building Recurring Revenue Streams with Membership Sites and Subscription Services

Membership sites and subscription services are two business concepts that can provide recurring and consistent revenue. They entail providing users with special materials, products, or services in exchange for a monthly charge. Let's take a look at membership sites and subscription services to see how they function and how you can use them to generate passive revenue.

Websites for Members:

1. A membership site is a password-protected online platform that provides paying members with access to unique material, resources, or a community. This is how it works:
2. Create high-quality, valuable material, resources, or services linked to a specific specialty or passion.
3. Create a Membership Site: To create a membership site, use website builders or specific membership site platforms such as MemberPress, Keerful, or Patrion.
4. **Gate material:** You restrict access to your premium material, ensuring that only paying members have access to it.
5. **Subscription Tiers:** Provide many levels of membership with differing levels of access or advantages. A basic tier, for example, may have access to unique articles, whereas a premium tier may contain additional services such as live webinars or personal coaching.
6. Set up a payment gateway to receive recurring membership fees from your members.
7. **Regular Content Updates:** Provide fresh and valuable content on a regular basis to retain and engage your members.

Benefits of Membership Websites:

1. **Recurring Revenue:** Subscription sites generate a consistent stream of money from subscribers who pay on an ongoing basis.
2. They generate a sense of belonging and community among individuals who have common interests.

3. Members have access to special content and resources that they cannot find anywhere else.
4. **Scalability:** As your membership base grows, so does your income potential.

Membership Website Difficulties:

1. **Material Commitment:** Creating valuable material on a consistent basis can be time-consuming.
2. **Member Retention:** It takes continual work to keep subscribers engaged and active.
3. **Customer Service:** You may need to provide assistance to members who have inquiries or problems.
4. Marketing: Attracting and converting new members might be difficult.
5. **Services by Subscription;** Subscription services involve providing a product or service for a recurring fee. It could be real items, digital goods, software, or service access. This is how it works:
6. Offering a Product or Service: You provide a product or service that appeals to a specific audience.
7. Subscription levels: Set up subscription levels with varying costs and advantages. A software-as-a-service (SaaS) platform, for example, may provide basic, premium, and enterprise plans.
8. Set up a method to collect regular payments, such as monthly or annual payments.
9. Customer Retention: Concentrate on retaining subscribers by meeting their requirements, addressing their complaints, and delivering good customer service.

Benefits of Subscription Services:

1. Subscription services provide a stable income stream through repeated payments.
2. Customer Loyalty: Subscribers are more inclined to stay, resulting in long-term customer connections.
3. Opportunities for Upselling: You can sell subscribers on higher-tier plans or additional products and services.
4. Product Feedback: Engaged subscribers can contribute valuable product feedback.

Subscription Services' Difficulties:

1. **Churn Rate:** If not managed properly, subscriber turnover (churn) can have an impact on income.
2. **Customer Acquisition:** Getting new subscribers can be expensive and difficult.
3. **Customer Expectations:** It is critical to meet customer expectations for constant value delivery in order to retain customers.
4. Membership Sites and Subscription Services That Work:
5. Netflix is a subscription-based streaming service with a large library of movies and television series.
6. Amazon Prime provides a variety of subscription services, such as Prime Video, Prime Music, and Prime Reading.
7. Spotify is a music streaming service that offers free and paid subscription tiers.
8. With various subscription plans, The New York Times provides digital access to news and premium content.
9. Platforms such as Reddit Premium and other specialty communities provide premium memberships with ad-free browsing and other perks.

Membership sites and subscription services can provide prospects for passive revenue, but success demands constant commitment, value delivery, and customer involvement. Whether you choose to construct a membership site or a subscription business, giving constant value to your customers is critical to creating a sustainable and profitable recurring revenue stream.

Chapter 4: Creating High-Quality Content

Content is king in the realm of online business and passive revenue. High-quality content not only attracts and engages your audience, but it also serves as the bedrock of your passive income strategy. This chapter discusses the significance of developing excellent content and offers tips on how to do so effectively.

Why high-quality content is important:

1. High-quality content captivates your audience, keeps them on your platform longer, and motivates them to come back for more.
2. **Credibility:** Outstanding content identifies you as an authority in your niche, fostering trust among your audience.
3. **Search engine presence:** higher ranks for excellent content are rewarded by search engines, enhancing your online presence.
4. **Shareability:** Well-crafted material is more likely to be shared on social media, thus expanding your reach and gaining new followers or customers.
5. **Monetization Potential:** Whether through advertisements, affiliate marketing, or product sales, quality content is the foundation of effective monetization tactics.

High-Quality Content Creation:

1. **Know Your Audience**: Before you develop content, research your target audience's wants, preferences, and pain areas. Make your material relevant to their needs and interests.
2. **Thorough Research:** Conduct thorough research on your selected topic. Make certain that your content is accurate, well-informed, and up-to-date.
3. Create attention-grabbing headlines that compel readers or viewers to click and investigate deeper.
4. **Clear framework:** For readability, organize your content with a clear framework that includes headings, subheadings, and bullet points.
5. **Engaging Visuals:** Include relevant images, infographics, or videos to increase the appeal of your material and efficiently deliver information.
6. **Originality:** To differentiate your content from competitors, provide a fresh perspective or take on the topic.

7. Develop a consistent voice and tone that resonates with your audience and is consistent with your brand.
8. **Proofreading and editing:** Edit and proofread your text thoroughly to eliminate errors and ensure readability.
9. **Optimize for SEO:** To boost search engine exposure, use on-page SEO tactics such as keyword research and optimization.
10. **Mobile-Friendly:** Make sure your content is accessible and responsive on a variety of devices, such as smartphones and tablets.

High-Quality Content Types:

1. **In-Depth Articles:** long-form articles that provide in-depth coverage of a subject.
2. **Videos:** video content that is engaging and educational, with clear visuals and narratives.
3. Podcasts are high-quality audio files that feature intelligent talks or interviews.
4. Infographics are visual representations of data or information that help to explain difficult topics.
5. **E-books:** comprehensive guides or books on certain topics that provide useful insights.
6. **How-To Guides and Tutorials:** Step-by-step instructions or tutorials that assist your audience in solving specific problems or achieving goals.

Consistency is essential.

When it comes to writing high-quality content for passive revenue, consistency is essential. Create and stick to a content schedule. Publishing material on a regular basis keeps your audience engaged and informed while also enhancing your search engine rankings. Aim for a mix of quality and frequency that is appropriate for your resources and goals.

Content Repurposing:

Repurposing information is an excellent way to maximize your efforts. Convert old content into new formats. Make a blog post into a video, podcast episode, or infographic, for example. This not only broadens the reach of your content but also caters to varied consumer preferences.

An effective passive income plan is built on the creation of high-quality content. You can establish a loyal following and lay the groundwork for revenue by understanding your audience, conducting rigorous research, and continually giving value. Keep in mind that the quality of your material indicates your dedication to your audience and is an important aspect of your long-term success.

Content Strategy and Planning

High-quality content is crucial, but careful planning and strategy can mean the difference between haphazard attempts and an organized, effective content marketing campaign. In this talk, we'll look at the significance of content planning and strategy, how to create them, and the essential elements for laying a good foundation.

Why content planning and strategy are important:

1. Planning and strategy Ensure that your material has a specific purpose, whether that objective is to educate, entertain, inspire, or convert.
2. **Consistency:** A content plan allows you to establish a consistent posting schedule, which keeps your audience engaged and coming back for more.
3. **Targeted Audience:** Strategies allow you to personalize information to the requirements, interests, and preferences of your target audience, enhancing its efficacy.
4. **Efficient content development:** A well-defined approach streamlines your content creation process, making it more efficient and time-consuming.
5. **Measurable Outcomes:** With a clear plan in place, you can create specific targets and key performance indicators (KPIs) to track the success of your content initiatives.

Creating a Content Strategy and Planning:

1. **Define Your Objectives:** Begin by defining your general goals. Do you want to raise brand awareness, create leads, enhance website traffic, or drive sales? Your content strategy will be guided by your objectives.
2. **Understand Your Audience:** Make thorough buyer personas for your target audience. Understand their pain spots, hobbies, and behaviors in order to generate content that is appealing to them.
3. **Content Audit:** If you already have content, conduct an audit to see what worked and what didn't. This aids in the identification of gaps and opportunities for improvement.
4. Conduct keyword research to uncover relevant subjects and phrases that your target audience is looking for. This helps with SEO by informing your content themes.

5. Create a content calendar defining when and what type of material you'll produce. Consider seasonality and industry patterns.
6. Decide on the types of material you'll produce, such as blog articles, videos, podcasts, infographics, or e-books.
7. **Content Distribution:** Determine how and where your content will be distributed. This includes your website, social media platforms, email newsletters, and any other channels that are relevant.
8. **Promotion Strategy:** Describe how you intend to promote your material in order to attract a larger audience. This could include social media advertising, influencer partnerships, or email marketing.
9. Create a workflow for content development that includes research, drafting, editing, and design. If you have a team, assign roles and duties.
10. **Measuring Success:** Create key performance indicators (KPIs) to track the efficacy of your content, such as website traffic, conversion rates, social media engagement, and email open rates.

Content Strategy Key Components:

1. **Content Voice and Tone:** Define your brand's voice and tone to maintain messaging consistency.
2. **Material Calendar:** Create a timetable for your material, including publication dates and subjects.
3. **Keyword Strategy:** In order to boost SEO and discoverability, use relevant keywords in your content.
4. Plan how and where you will market your content to reach your target audience.
5. **Material Repurposing:** Look for ways to repurpose material into different formats to reach a larger audience.
6. Develop techniques for interacting with your audience via comments, social media, or email.
7. **Competitor Analysis:** Monitor your competitors' content initiatives to uncover opportunities and remain ahead of the competition.
8. **Budget and Resources:** Set aside funds for content creation, promotion, and tools, if necessary.

Evolve and adapt:

A dynamic content strategy and planning should allow for revisions based on performance and changes in your industry or audience preferences. To effectively reach your goals, examine the impact of your material on a regular basis, obtain feedback, and change your strategy accordingly.

Finally, content strategy and preparation are critical for developing meaningful, consistent, and profitable content that supports your online business and passive income activities. You may design a path to content success that provides long-term advantages by analyzing your goals, audience, and resources, as well as adopting best practices.

Writing engaging blog posts

Blogging is an effective way to share information, share your skills, and interact with your audience. In a sea of blog entries, however, it's critical to stand out by providing intriguing material that keeps readers coming back for more. Here's how to produce blog entries that will attract and hold your readers' interest.

1. Understand Your Audience:

Understanding your intended audience is critical. Consider their demographics, interests, problems, and goals. Customize your content to meet their needs and tastes.

2. Select Interesting Topics:

Choose themes that are interesting to your target audience. Look for hot topics, address frequently asked questions, or delve into specialist areas of interest. Make sure your topics are related to the main theme or specialty of your site.

3. Create Engaging Headlines:

Your headline is the first thing readers notice about your piece. Make it appealing, concise, and fascinating. To spark interest, use power words, questions, or statistics.

4. Begin with a Hook:

The first paragraph should hook your readers and persuade them to keep reading. Tell a compelling story, shocking fact, or provocative inquiry about your topic.

5. Organize Your Content:

Use clear headings, subheadings, and bullet points to organize your blog article. This format makes your material scannable and consumable, which keeps readers interested.

6. Offer Value:

Provide your readers with useful information, insights, or solutions. Provide actionable advice, helpful hints, or in-depth analysis that meets their concerns or interests.

7. Include Visuals:

Break up the text with photographs, infographics, videos, or bespoke visuals to improve your message. Visuals increase the engagement and shareability of your content.

8. Employ Engaging Language:

As if you were speaking to a buddy, write in a conversational tone. Avoid using jargon or unnecessarily complicated terminology. Be brief and to the point.

9. Tell a Story:

Stories personalize and relatable your content. Use personal tales, case studies, or real-life examples to demonstrate your views and emotionally connect with your audience.

10. Data and statistics should be included:

Data, statistics, and research should be used to back up your arguments. This increases the trustworthiness of your information and strengthens your arguments.

11. Promote Interaction:

Ask questions, invite comments, or hold polls to keep your audience interested. Encourage them to leave comments with their opinions and experiences.

12. SEO optimization:

To boost search engine exposure, conduct keyword research and naturally incorporate important terms into your content. However, readability and user experience should always come first.

13. Be Brief:

While giving value is crucial, keep in mind the length of your blog article. Strive for a mix of depth and brevity. Consider your readers' time.

14. Editing and Proofreading:

Grammar and spelling errors can detract from the quality of your material. Edit your blog content thoroughly to guarantee clarity and accuracy.

15. Add a Call to Action (CTA) at the end:

Finish your blog post with a clear call to action. Guide your readers on what to do next, whether it's subscribing to your newsletter, sharing the piece, or doing a specific action.

16.Share Your Personal Insights:

Share your distinct point of view, views, and insights. Your voice and experiences give your article authenticity.

17. Iterate and test:

Take note of reader feedback and analytics. To find out what works best for your audience, experiment with different writing styles, content types, and techniques.

18. Maintain Consistency:

Building a readership requires consistency. Maintain a consistent posting schedule so that readers know when to expect new information.

Keep in mind that creating interesting blog posts is a continuous process of learning and improvement. As you try new approaches and respond to your audience's criticism, you'll refine your talents and become a more fascinating blogger, gaining a loyal following along the way.

Producing videos and podcasts

Making Videos and Podcasts: How to Create Engaging Visual and Audio Content

Video and podcasting have evolved as very powerful methods for transmitting information, storytelling, and engaging audiences in the digital age. Producing videos and podcasts can be a satisfying effort, whether you're an entrepreneur wanting to build your internet presence or someone with a passion to share. Let's look at the realm of visual and audio content creation and how to do it well.

Making Videos:

1. Videos are an exciting and interactive method to communicate with your audience. Here are the fundamental elements to generating interesting videos, whether you're creating tutorials, vlogs, interviews, or storytelling content:
2. **Planning and scripting:** Make a detailed plan first. Define your intended audience, goals, and message. To ensure a flawless delivery, script your material.
3. Invest in high-quality equipment, such as a camera, microphone, lighting, and editing software. Create a clean, well-lit filming setting.
4. **Filming:** Capture your movie with crisp audio and bright graphics. Keep your eyes on the camera and speak clearly.
5. **Editing:** To improve your footage, use video editing software. Remove unneeded portions, add images, and improve audio quality. Maintain a consistent aesthetic throughout.
6. **Engaging Thumbnails and Titles:** To attract visitors, create eye-catching video thumbnails and captivating titles.
7. Upload your film to platforms like YouTube, Vimeo, or social media for publication and promotion. Use email newsletters, social media, and collaborations with influencers or other creators to promote your work.
8. **Engage Your Audience:** Interact with your audience via comments and social media. Respond to comments and questions, and create a community around your material.

Making Podcasts:

1. Podcasting provides a one-of-a-kind platform for audio storytelling, interviews, and debates. Here's how to make interesting podcasts:
2. Think about your podcast's niche, format, and themes. Outline episodes and, if applicable, guest suggestions.
3. Invest in a high-quality microphone, headphones, and audio recording/editing software. Make sure you have a quiet recording space.
4. **Script or Outline:** To preserve structure and flow, plan your episodes with a script or outline. When appropriate, allow for spontaneous conversations.
5. **Recording:** To ensure great audio quality, record your podcast. Take note of your tempo, tone, and energy levels.
6. **Editing:** Remove background noise, pauses, and typos from your audio. Improve the audio quality by adding intro/outro music or effects.
7. **Cover Art and Titles:** Create eye-catching cover art and descriptive episode titles that pique the interest of potential listeners.
8. **Hosting and distribution:** To save your episodes, select a podcast hosting site (e.g., Libyan, Pod bean). Distribute your podcast through services such as Apple Podcasts, Spotify, Google Podcasts, and others.
9. **Promotion:** Use social media, your website, email marketing, and collaborations with other podcasters or influencers to promote your podcast.
10. Encourage feedback, evaluations, and queries from your listeners. Consider using social media or a dedicated website to build a community around your podcast.

Success Hints:

1. Maintain a consistent posting schedule for both videos and podcasts to keep your audience engaged and coming back for more.
2. Prioritize the quality of your material over the quantity of episodes or videos that you produce.
3. **Storytelling:** Whether in video or podcast form, storytelling is an effective approach to emotionally engage your audience and produce memorable content.

4. Pay attention to listener/viewer input and adjust your content accordingly.
5. **Collaboration:** To extend your audience and bring fresh viewpoints, collaborate with other creators, guests, or professionals in your sector.
6. Monetization alternatives include sponsorships, affiliate marketing, merchandising, and even special content for subscribers.

Keep in mind that success in video and podcast production typically requires patience and perseverance. You'll discover your own voice and style as you grow your audience and develop your content, creating content that resonates with your viewers and listeners and potentially converting your passion into a profitable online company.

Building an Email List

Building an email list is a critical tool in the realm of internet business and content development. It's a direct line of communication with your target audience, a potent marketing tool, and a way to cultivate relationships and generate engagement. Here's how to properly grow and leverage your email list, whether you're a blogger, business, or content provider.

1. Create Useful Content:

Offering value to your audience is the core of email list building. Produce high-quality material, whether it's in the form of blog entries, videos, podcasts, or downloadable resources. People are more likely to subscribe if they feel your content valuable.

2. Selecting an Email Marketing Service:

Choose a trustworthy email marketing solution, such as Mailchimp, Convert Kit, A Weber, or Constant Contact. These platforms include list management, automation, and campaign tracking tools.

3. Put in place opt-in forms:

Strategically place opt-in forms on your website or content channels. Typical sites include:

- Forms that pop up
- Widgets for the sidebar
- Throughout blog postings or material
- Page landings
- Pop-ups with an exit intent

4. Provide Incentives:

Encourage visitors to sign up by providing excellent incentives such as:

- Whitepapers or e-books
- Guides or exclusive content
- Coupons or discounts
- Registration for webinars or courses

- Free resources or templates

5. Create Captivating CTAs:

Create clear and appealing calls to action (CTAs) to entice visitors to sign up. Make use of appealing wording and eye-catching placement.

6. Divide Your List:

Subscribers can be segmented depending on their interests, activity, or demographics as your list expands. This enables you to send tailored and relevant content, resulting in increased interaction.

7. Show Social Proof:

To develop trust with potential subscribers, display testimonials, reviews, or the number of subscribers you have.

8. Make Use of Landing Pages:

Make specific landing pages for campaigns or lead magnets. These pages are purely intended to collect email addresses and can be extremely effective.

9. Organize Webinars or Events:

Hosting webinars, virtual events, or workshops is a great approach to gather email addresses. Registration is required to participate.

Organize contests and giveaways:

Contests and giveaways can quickly expand your mailing list. Encourage people to enter their email addresses in order to be eligible for rewards.

11. Make use of social media:

To reach a larger audience, promote your lead magnets and opt-in forms on social media.

12. Work Together with Others:

Collaborate with influencers and other content providers to cross-promote your lead magnets or subscription offers to their respective audiences.

13. Produce Shareable Content:

Create highly shareable content to expand its exposure and possibilities for email address collection.

14. Keep Transparency:

Make it obvious to subscribers what they may expect when they join your list. Inform them about your email frequency and the type of content they will get.

15. Send Interesting Emails:

Focus on sending engaging, valuable emails once you've developed your list. To increase open rates, personalize your content and utilize intriguing subject lines.

16. Test and Improve:

To optimize your campaigns, assess your email performance on a regular basis and run A/B testing on subject lines, content, and CTAs.

17. Obey privacy laws:

To ensure that you are handling subscriber data responsibly, follow data protection rules such as GDPR or CAN-SPAM.

18.Relationship Nurturing:

Building an email list entail more than just gathering addresses; it also entails fostering relationships. Continue to add value, listen to your subscribers, and interact with them.

19. Calculate ROI:

Monitor indicators like as open rates, click-through rates, conversion rates, and revenue generated to determine the return on investment (ROI) of your email marketing initiatives.

It takes time and work to build an email list, but the benefits of having a direct line of communication with your audience are enormous. It enables you to cultivate loyalty, drive traffic, market products or services, and, ultimately, generate passive money by effectively connecting with your subscribers.

Chapter 5: Monetization Strategies for Passive Income

Now that you've established the foundation for your online passive income business, it's time to investigate alternative monetization tactics that can turn your efforts into a long-term money stream. This chapter digs into tried-and-true strategies for monetizing your internet presence and increasing your earnings.

1. Advertising Income:

Advertising is one of the most frequent techniques of monetization. You can earn money by displaying adverts on your website, blog, or YouTube channel using one of the following models:

- **Pay-Per-Click (PPC):** When a visitor clicks on an ad displayed on your platform, you earn money. Google AdSense is a well-known pay-per-click (PPC) advertising network.
- **CPM:** You are paid a certain amount for every thousand ad impressions (views) on your content. CPM rates might vary significantly.
- **CPA:** This model rewards you when a user performs a certain action after clicking an ad, such as completing a purchase or signing up for a newsletter.
- **Sponsored Content:** Collaborate with marketers to create sponsored posts, videos, or mentions relevant to your niche and audience.

2. Affiliate Promotion:

Affiliate marketing entails advertising products or services in exchange for a commission on each sale or action created by your recommendation. The following are important steps in affiliate marketing success:

- **Choosing Relevant Products:** Choose products or services that are relevant to your target audience and specialty.
- **Transparent Promotion:** To preserve confidence with your audience, clearly disclose your affiliate ties.
- **Quality Content:** To promote conversions, create useful and persuasive content.

1. **Effective Tracking:** Use tracking links and tools to monitor the performance of your affiliates.

3. Digital Goods:

Use your knowledge to generate and sell digital products like e-books, online courses, templates, or digital art. Once designed and efficiently marketed, these goods can provide a passive income stream.

- **Membership Sites:** Place premium content, resources, or a community forum behind a paywall to entice subscribers to pay for exclusive access. Develop and market software solutions or digital tools that solve specific demands within your specialty.
- **Sponsorships and Brand Alliances:** Work with brands or firms in your niche to create sponsored content, product placements, or brand endorsements. Negotiate pay depending on your impact and reach.

5. Subscription Plans:

Create subscription-based services or content in which users pay a monthly or yearly charge for access to premium resources, exclusive material, or continuing assistance. Popular platforms include Patrion, Sub stack, and private membership sites.

6.Drop shipping and eCommerce:

Consider drop shipping if you sell physical things or have an online store to reduce inventory management. Concentrate on specialty products that are relevant to your target audience's interests.

7. Donations and crowdsourcing:

Allow your audience to support your work by making one-time payments (e.g., through PayPal) or by using crowdfunding platforms such as Kickstarter or Indiegogo. Engage your supporters by providing incentives or prizes.

8. Coaching and consultation:

Make use of your skills to provide consulting or coaching services. Give one-on-one advice, workshops, or webinars on issues related to your niche.

9.Merchandise and branded goods:

Create and sell branded stuff like T-shirts, mugs, posters, or digital products that appeal to your target demographic.

10.Syndication and Licensing:

In exchange for royalties or syndication fees, you can license your material, such as images, articles, or videos, to other platforms or media sources.

11.Real Estate and Investing:

To generate passive revenue streams outside of your web business, invest in income-generating assets such as rental properties, stocks, or dividend-paying investments.

Remember that income diversification is critical for long-term success. It is dangerous to rely entirely on one type of revenue. Combine different tactics to build a robust and durable passive income environment that fits your niche, audience, and business objectives.

Affiliate Marketing Strategies

Affiliate marketing is a strong technique to produce passive money by advertising products or services and receiving referral commissions. To be successful in affiliate marketing, you must use smart tactics that increase your earnings while preserving your audience's confidence. Here are some affiliate marketing tactics to help you succeed:

1. Select the Correct Products and Markets:

Choose affiliate products or services that are relevant to your specialty and audience. Choose products that you truly believe in and that your target audience would find useful. Relevance is essential for affiliate marketing success.

2. Increase trust and credibility:

Establish yourself as a credible authority in your field. Provide useful information, ideas, and unbiased evaluations. Your audience should trust your recommendations since they know you are looking out for their best interests.

3. Identify Affiliate Relationships:

Be open and honest about your affiliate relationships. Make it clear that you may receive a commission if users purchase through your affiliate links. Honesty fosters trust and keeps your credibility.

4.Make High-Quality Content:

Create material that is useful, entertaining, and well-researched. Share in-depth product evaluations, tutorials, comparisons, or case studies that will assist your audience in making educated judgments.

5. Use Appealing Visuals:

Incorporate eye-catching photos, videos, and infographics to increase the appeal of your information. Visuals can help you explain the value and benefits of the products you're promoting more effectively.

6. Use SEO Best Practices:

Conduct keyword research and strategically place keywords in your content to optimize it for search engines. SEO may increase the visibility of your affiliate content by helping it rank higher in search results.

7. Split Testing:

Experiment with various affiliate methods, such as adjusting the positioning and style of affiliate links, call-to-action (CTA) buttons, and the wording of your recommendations. A/B testing assists in determining what is most appealing to your target audience.

8. Strategically Promote Affiliate Offers:

Take into account the context and timing of your affiliate advertising. Promotions should be coordinated with relevant information, such as product reviews or buying advice. Profit from seasonal trends, special promotions, or new product releases.

9. Make use of email marketing:

Make the most of your email list to promote affiliate items. Create convincing email campaigns that showcase the items' worth and benefits. To target subscribers with certain interests, segment your list.

10. Leverage the Power of social media:

Distribute your affiliate links on social media. Create interesting postings, tales, or films that explain how the products solve problems or improve people's lives.

11. Use retargeting and remarketing techniques:

Use retargeting and remarketing methods to reconnect with visitors who interacted with your content but did not convert. Show advertisements to remind customers of the things you've recommended.

12. Maintain Knowledge and Adapt:

The affiliate marketing landscape is ever-changing. Keep up with industry trends, new affiliate programs, and regulatory changes. Prepare to modify your strategies as needed.

13. Expand Affiliate Programs:

Join several affiliate schemes to diversify your earnings. Various programs provide varying commission schemes, items, and terms. Diversification can minimize risk while increasing overall earnings.

14. Performance Monitoring and Analysis:

Track the performance of your affiliate campaigns on a regular basis. Metrics like as click-through rates, conversion rates, and earnings per click should be examined. Use this information to fine-tune your strategy and zero in on what works best.

15.Develop Long-Term Relationships:

Maintain contact with your affiliate partners. As your influence rises, communicate effectively, seek exclusive offers for your audience, and negotiate greater commission rates.

16. Maintain Ethical and Legal Compliance:

Follow ethical affiliate marketing techniques and regulations such as the Federal Trade Commission (FTC) rules. Deceptive or misleading practices can hurt your reputation.

Remember that success in affiliate marketing often takes time and persistence. Building a dedicated following and improving your techniques take time. You may develop a sustained and lucrative passive income stream through affiliate marketing by combining these approaches with effort and a commitment to offering value.

E-commerce Optimization

In the highly competitive world of e-commerce, optimization is essential for standing out, attracting customers, and increasing revenue. These tactics will help you optimize your operations and achieve success whether you run a tiny online business or manage a massive e-commerce network.

1. Convenient Website Design:

The design and style of your website should be simple and easy to use. Ensure simple navigation, distinct product categories, and a responsive design that works on both desktop and mobile platforms.

2. Checkout Process Simplified:

Make the checkout procedure as easy and quick as feasible. Reduce the number of steps necessary to complete a purchase and provide guest checkout options. Reduce basket abandonment by removing distractions from the checkout page.

3. Product images and descriptions of high quality:

High-resolution photos and full product descriptions should be provided. Include many photographs from different perspectives, as well as videos if possible. Customers can make more educated judgments when they have access to accurate and thorough information.

4. Quick Loading Speed:

Improve the loading speed of your website. Slow websites can irritate visitors and increase bounce rates. To increase performance, compress pictures, remove unneeded plugins, and employ content delivery networks (CDNs).

5. SEO (Search Engine Optimization):

Improve your website's search engine ranks by implementing on-page and off-page SEO methods. Optimize product titles, descriptions, and meta tags, and prioritize the creation of high-quality backlinks.

6. Optimization for Mobile Devices:

Given the growing number of mobile buyers, optimizing your e-commerce site for mobile devices is critical. Make sure your website is responsive and offers a consistent experience across smartphones and tablets.

7. Customer Feedback and Ratings:

Encourage customers to offer feedback and ratings on the things they've purchased. Positive feedback fosters trust and credibility, whilst negative feedback provides suggestions for improvement.

8. Individualization:

Personalization elements that adjust product recommendations and content to individual customer preferences should be implemented. This has the potential to increase engagement and conversion rates.

9.Secure Payment Methods:

Provide a number of safe payment choices, such as credit cards, digital wallets, and alternative payment methods such as PayPal. Check that payment methods are secure and secured.

10. Inventory Control:

To avoid overselling and stockouts, keep precise inventory levels. Implement inventory tracking and replenishment solutions to improve the efficiency of your supply chain.

11.Email Marketing:

Email marketing can be used to engage customers, offer personalized product recommendations, and perform focused promotional efforts. Potential sales can also be recovered with abandoned cart emails.

12. Integration of social media:

Connect your e-commerce business to social networking platforms. Allow clients to use their social network profiles to log in or make transactions. Use social media to promote your products and engage your customers.

13. Split Testing:

Conduct A/B tests on a regular basis to improve various aspects of your e-commerce site, such as product descriptions, photos, CTAs, and pricing. Data-driven decisions can result in better performance.

14. Customer Service:

Provide outstanding customer service over several channels, including live chat, email, and phone. Respond to consumer concerns and issues as soon as possible to increase trust and satisfaction.

15. Data Analytics and Insights:

Track user behavior, sales trends, and conversion rates with analytics tools. Make data-driven decisions and optimize your marketing campaigns with these insights.

16.Optimization of Shipping and Returns:

Provide affordable shipping costs, quick delivery alternatives, and a clear return policy. Shipping costs and return procedures have a significant impact on customer satisfaction.

17.Loyalty Programs:

To encourage repeat purchases, implement loyalty programs or reward schemes. Customers that feel valued and rewarded are more inclined to return.

18. Marketing through several channels:

To reach a larger audience, diversify your marketing efforts by utilizing numerous channels such as social media advertising, search engine marketing, and email campaigns.

19. Constant Improvement:

E-commerce optimization is a continuous procedure. Analyze your performance indicators on a regular basis, collect consumer feedback, and respond to shifting market trends and customer preferences.

Keep in mind that optimization is not a one-size-fits-all solution. Make your strategy unique to your company, audience, and goals. You can create a smooth shopping experience that inspires client loyalty and generates revenue development by constantly optimizing your e-commerce operations.

Leveraging advertising and sponsorships

Advertising and sponsorships are two effective ways to monetize your online presence, whether you have a blog, a social network account, a YouTube channel, or any other type of content platform. These tactics can help you make cash while preserving your audience's trust and involvement. Let's look at ways to make the most of advertising and sponsorships:

Advertising:

1. **Google AdSense and Related Programs:** Google AdSense is a well-known platform that allows you to display tailored advertisements on your website or content. When visitors click on these adverts, you earn money. Focus on content that is relevant to your audience and optimize ad placement for increased click-through rates to maximize earnings.
2. **Display Advertising Networks:** Look into additional display advertising networks like Media.net, Ad Thrive, or Eozoic, which have competitive pricing and a variety of ad types. Try out many networks to find the one that best suits your audience and content.
3. Native advertising blends in with your content, delivering a more natural user experience. Native advertising solutions are provided by platforms such as Taboola and Outbrain. To preserve authenticity, ensure that native ads correspond with your content.
4. While affiliate marketing was previously covered, it's worth noting that promoting affiliate products through banner advertisements or text links within your content can be a profitable advertising approach. Make certain that the products are relevant and truly valuable to your target audience.
5. **Ad Blocker Detection:** Some users use ad blockers, which might reduce your advertising earnings. Use ad blocker detection tools to ask people to disable ad blocks or subscribe to an ad-free version of your site.

Sponsorships:

1. **Identify Compatible Partners:** When looking for sponsorships, look for brands or firms that fit your specialty and resonate with your target audience. Ensure that the sponsors' products or services are relevant to your content.

2. **Proactively engage brands:** Don't wait for sponsors to approach you; instead, take the initiative. Send a well-crafted proposal to potential sponsors that highlights your audience demographics, engagement analytics, and the benefits of collaborating with your platform.
3. **Transparent Disclosure:** Maintain transparency by explicitly declaring to your audience your sponsorship affiliations. These fosters trust and assures adherence to regulations and norms, such as those issued by the Federal Trade Commission (FTC).
4. **bespoke Campaigns:** Collaborate closely with sponsors to create bespoke campaigns that seamlessly integrate their products or services into your content. Instead of overtly promotional or obtrusive content, focus on providing value to your audience.
5. **Measure and Report Results:** Provide thorough performance reports to sponsors that demonstrate the impact of their sponsorship. Metrics such as engagement rates, click-through rates, and conversions can illustrate the partnership's efficacy.
6. **Long-Term Partnerships:** Develop long-term relationships with sponsors whenever possible. Collaborations with trusted companies on a regular basis can result in consistent income and long-term relationships.
7. **Negotiate Fair remuneration:** When negotiating fair remuneration for your sponsored content, consider aspects such as the size of your audience, engagement rates, and the breadth of the campaign. Avoid undervaluing your worth.

Monetization against Audience Experience:

1. While advertising and sponsorships are necessary for income generation, it is critical to achieve a balance between monetization and audience experience. Here are some pointers to avoid alienating your audience during your monetization efforts:
2. Prioritize excellent content and user experience over quantity. Avoid clogging your platform with too many adverts or sponsorships that interrupt the user experience.
3. **Engage and communicate with your audience**: Maintain an open line of communication with them. Adjust your methods in response to their complaints or feedback about advertising or sponsored material.

4. **Transparency:** Be open and honest about your monetization strategies and collaborations. Your audience will value candor and genuineness.
5. **Relevance:** To prevent alienating your followers, make sure that your adverts and sponsorships are relevant to your specialty and audience interests.
6. **Testing and Feedback:** Test various advertising and sponsoring tactics on a regular basis to measure audience reactions. Improve your monetization methods with feedback and statistics.

Finally, monetizing your internet presence with advertising and sponsorships might be a successful option. You may create a win-win situation for both your audience and your income goals by adhering to ethical principles, preserving openness, and prioritizing the user experience.

Membership site revenue

Operating a membership site can be a lucrative method to monetize your knowledge, material, or community. Whether you're an educator, content provider, or specialty enthusiast, producing cash through membership sites provides a number of advantages, including regular income and a dedicated audience. Here's how you efficiently use membership sites to generate revenue:

1. Provide Unique Value:

To persuade people to join, offer exclusive content, resources, or experiences that cannot be accessed elsewhere. Your membership's perceived benefit should outweigh the cost.

2. Select the Appropriate Platform:

Choose a membership site platform that is compatible with your objectives and target audience. WordPress with membership plugins (e.g., MemberPress, Restrict Content Pro), dedicated membership site builders (e.g., Kajaki, Teachable), and even social media platforms like patron are popular possibilities.

3. Pricing Policy:

Determine your price approach based on the depth and distinctiveness of your material. Provide tiers of membership, with each tier having distinct benefits and access. Consider monthly, yearly, or lifetime subscriptions.

4. Content Diversification:

Diversify your material to appeal to a diverse audience. Exclusive articles, films, webinars, downloadable tools, or a private community forum may be included. Update content on a regular basis to keep members interested.

5. Participation in the Community:

Encourage your members to have a sense of belonging. Encourage private community discussions, networking, and knowledge exchange. Members who are actively involved are more inclined to renew their memberships.

6. Special Events:

Host unique live webinars, Q&A sessions, or virtual events for subscribers. These events provide value and foster a sense of belonging.

7. Combination of free and paid content:

Provide a mix of free and member-only content. Encourage conversions by attracting new users with free material and subsequently highlighting the value of premium content.

8. Discounts and Early Access:

Members should be given first access to new material or product launches. Provide special discounts on merchandise, courses, or other products you may sell.

9. Member Comments:

Solicit input from your members to better understand their wants and requirements. Use this data to adapt your content and offerings to better match their needs.

10. Promotion and marketing:

Promote your membership site using numerous methods, such as your website, social media, email marketing, and collaborations with industry influencers or partners.

11. Money-Back Guarantees and Trial Periods:

To reduce the risk for potential members, consider offering trial periods or money-back guarantees. This can persuade apprehensive visitors to join your club.

12.Analytics and Optimization:

Track member engagement, subscription trends, and churn rates with analytics tools. Analyze this information to optimize your content strategy and member retention.

13.Affiliate Programs:

Create an affiliate program to encourage current members to suggest others. For successful referrals, reward them with discounts or commissions.

14. Reliable Communication:

Keep in touch with your members on a regular basis by sending out newsletters, updates, and announcements. Keep them up to date on new content and forthcoming events.

15. Member Assistance:

Provide exceptional customer service to handle any difficulties or complaints your members may have as soon as possible. Members who are satisfied are more inclined to renew their subscriptions.

16. Increase Revenue Stream Diversification:

Consider other revenue streams to supplement your membership income, such as retail sales, online courses, or consultancy services.

17. Check and Adjust:

Monitor the operation of your membership site on a regular basis and solicit input from members. Be open to modifying your plan based on what works best for your target audience.

Remember that it takes time and work to develop a successful membership site and generate consistent revenue. It is critical to concentrate on giving continual value to your members and building a flourishing community. You can transform your membership site into a sustainable source of money while cultivating a loyal and engaged audience by doing so.

Chapter 6: Automating Your Online Business

In the realm of internet enterprises, automation is a major changer. It enables you to simplify operations, save time, and concentrate on strategic growth. In this chapter, we'll look at how to automate your internet business for efficiency and scalability.

1. Automated Email Marketing:

Email marketing is a wonderful tool for communicating with your audience, but it may be difficult to manage manually. Email marketing automation tools such as Mailchimp, Convert Kit, or Active Campaign can be used to:

- Create automated email sequences for lead nurturing, onboarding, and post-purchase follow-ups.
- Divide your email list into segments depending on user behavior, interests, or demographics.
- Send tailored product suggestions and content.
- Email marketing should be A/B tested for optimization.
- Schedule emails automatically to reach your audience at the optimal moments.

2. Scheduling social media:

Online firms must maintain a consistent social media presence. Buffer, Hootsuite, and Later are social media management platforms that can assist you:

- Schedule postings across various platforms in advance.
- Create a content calendar by planning and curating content.
- A unified dashboard allows you to monitor and interact with your audience.
- Examine performance analytics to help you fine-tune your social media approach.

3. Publishing and Content Management:

It is critical to manage your website's content efficiently. WordPress and other content management systems (CMS) provide plugins and tools to:

- Plan your blog entries and material updates.
- Automate the distribution of material via social media and email newsletters.
- Create content approval protocols for your teams.
- Keep an eye on the website's performance and security.

4. Automated E-commerce:

Automation may dramatically improve productivity in e-commerce businesses:

- To handle inventory, track orders, and process payments automatically, use e-commerce platforms like Shopify or WooCommerce.
- Implement abandoned cart email recovery processes.
- Set up autoresponders for customer assistance and questions.
- Integrate with shipping and fulfillment services to ensure that orders are processed smoothly.

5.CRM (Customer Relationship Management):

CRM software, such as Salesforce, HubSpot, or Soho, can assist you in managing customer interactions and automating:

- Tracking and developing leads.
- Email correspondence with leads and customers.
- Management of the sales pipeline and follow-up.
- Ticketing and resolution for customer assistance.

6.Automation of Finance and Accounting:

Accounting and financial management can be time-consuming. Automation software such as QuickBooks or Xero can:

- Invoice and payment reminders can be automated.
- Keep track of your expenses and generate financial reports.
- Connect your bank accounts for real-time financial information.

7. Chatbots and customer service:

Integrate chatbots or AI-powered customer care systems to deliver rapid responses to frequently asked questions from customers. This can enhance the user experience while also reducing the workload on your support personnel.

8.Reporting and analytics:

Using analytics and reporting tools such as Google Analytics or Data Studio, you can:

- Gather and analyze website traffic statistics automatically.
- Create performance reports and analytics.
- Create personalized notifications for critical metrics.

9. Project and Task Management:

Tools such as Trello, Asana, and Monday.com can assist you in automating project management:

- Assign team members tasks and deadlines.
- Keep track of the project's progress and milestones.
- Task reminders and notifications can be automated.

10.Automated Marketing and Advertising:

Use marketing automation tools such as Market or HubSpot to:

- Lead scoring and nurturing can be automated.
- Plan and optimize digital advertising initiatives.
- Audiences should be segmented and targeted for tailored marketing.

11.Management of Affiliates and Partnerships:

Automate monitoring, commissions, and payments for firms that deal with affiliates or partners to streamline these interactions.

- Backup and security are also important considerations.
- To safeguard your online business from data loss and cyber dangers, automate frequent data backups and security scans.

13. Customer Surveys and Feedback:

Gather client feedback and run surveys automatically to acquire insights and improve your products or services.

14. Legal and Regulatory Compliance:

Use automation to ensure legal and regulatory compliance, such as data protection and privacy legislation.

15. Scaling and Expansion:

Consider automating tasks linked to hiring, onboarding, and training new team members as your online business grows.

Automation is a continuous process that changes along with your company. Continuously evaluate your processes and look for new automation solutions to increase productivity, improve customer experiences, and free up time to focus on strategic projects and growth. You can maximize the possibilities of your internet business by embracing automation.

The importance of automation

Automation has become an essential component of modern corporate operations in a variety of industries. It entails using technology and software to conduct time-consuming, repetitive operations with minimum human participation. Automation's importance cannot be emphasized, as it provides several benefits that contribute to efficiency, production, cost-effectiveness, and competitiveness. Here are some of the main reasons why automation is so important in today's corporate landscape:

1. Automation improves efficiency by decreasing the need for manual intervention. It reduces human-caused errors and ensures activities are completed consistently and accurately. This efficiency results in shorter turnaround times, better resource allocation, and increased output.
2. **Cost Savings:** Automating routine operations and procedures lowers the labor expenses associated with manual labor. It also reduces costs associated with human errors, such as rework and quality control. While there may be some initial costs associated with introducing automation, the long-term savings are significant.
3. Automation enables organizations to operate around the clock without the need for constant human oversight. This is especially useful for customer assistance, e-commerce, and key infrastructure, guaranteeing that services are always available to a global audience.
4. **Scalability:** As a company grows, automation allows it to extend its processes without increasing its labor accordingly. This adaptability is critical for dealing with changes in demand and expanding into new areas.
5. **Improved Customer Experience:** Automation can improve customer service by responding to requests quickly, resolving issues quickly, and personalizing interactions. Tools that improve the customer experience include chatbots, automated emails, and self-service portals.
6. Automation tools collect and analyze massive volumes of data, allowing businesses to make informed decisions. Based on data insights, machine learning algorithms may spot trends, forecast future events, and enhance operations.
7. Automation guarantees that processes are done consistently in accordance with predetermined rules and standards. This is

especially important in areas with stringent regulatory standards, such as healthcare, finance, and manufacturing.

8. Employees can focus on higher-value activities that involve creativity, problem-solving, and strategic thinking by automating repetitive processes. As a result, employees are more engaged and happier.
9. **Advantage:** Businesses that adopt automation have a competitive advantage. They can offer products and services more effectively, react to market changes more swiftly, and innovate more quickly than their competitors.
10. **Adaptability:** Automation can be adjusted to specific business requirements and evolve as those requirements change. This adaptability enables firms to remain nimble in a constantly changing business environment.
11. Automation minimizes the possibility of human errors, which can result in costly blunders or security breaches. It also includes backup and recovery procedures to protect vital data and operations.
12. **Environmental Impact:** Automating operations can result in lower energy consumption, fewer paper consumption, and more sustainable practices, all of which contribute to a company's environmental responsibility and minimize its carbon footprint.
13. **Global Collaboration:** Automation systems make it easier for geographically distributed teams to collaborate. They offer real-time communication, file sharing, and project management, fostering cross-border collaboration.

To summarize, automation has changed the way businesses run by increasing efficiency, decreasing costs, improving consumer experiences, and enabling innovation. As technology advances, the relevance of automation will only increase, making it a necessary component for businesses seeking to flourish in the digital age. Embracing automation may help you stay competitive, nimble, and future-ready, whether you're a small company or a major enterprise.

Automation Tools and Platforms

Automation is a great tool for streamlining company operations, saving time, and increasing efficiency. To properly implement automation, the right tools and platforms are required. Here are some tools and platforms from many categories to help you automate work and increase productivity:

1. Automation of Workflows:

- **Zapier:** Zapier connects apps and automates workflows by establishing "Zaps" that trigger actions when specified events occur across many apps.
- **Integrate:** Provides advanced automation by linking numerous apps, APIs, and services, enabling complicated workflows.
- **Microsoft Power Automate:** Previously known as Microsoft Flow, it automates tasks within the Microsoft ecosystem and interfaces with hundreds of other applications.

2. Automated Email Marketing:

- **Mailchimp:** Mailchimp is a well-known email marketing software that automates email marketing campaigns, audience segmentation, and reporting.
- **Active Campaign:** Offers complex email automation tools such as behavioral triggers, lead scoring, and CRM integration.
- **Convert Kit:** Designed for creators, it provides email sequence automation, subscriber tagging, and personalized emails.

3. Automation of social media:

- **Buffer:** Allows for the scheduling and automation of social media postings across many platforms, as well as performance metrics.
- **Hootsuite:** Provides tools for managing various social profiles, including social media scheduling, engagement, and reporting.
- **Later:** Specializing in Instagram scheduling and visual content planning, with automated posting and analytics capabilities.

4. Blog Automation and Content Management:

- **WordPress:** The CMS provides plugins such as WP Scheduled Posts for content automation and Editorial Calendar for content planning.
- **HubSpot CMS:** Offers content automation tools such as SEO optimization and content recommendations.

5.CRM (Customer Relationship Management):

- **Salesforce:** A comprehensive CRM platform with sales, marketing, and customer support automation capabilities.
- **HubSpot CRM:** Provides free CRM software with lead management, email tracking, and contact nurturing automation tools.

6. Sales Automation and E-commerce:

- **Shopify:** Shopify is an e-commerce platform that provides automated inventory management, order processing, and cart recovery.
- **WooCommerce:** A WordPress plugin that automates online shop e-commerce, including product administration and sales tracking.

7. Task Automation and Project Management:

- **Trello:** Trello is a visual project management tool that connects with automation platforms such as Butler to automate tasks.
- **Asana:** Provides task and project automation solutions to improve project efficiency and communication.

8.Automation in Marketing and Advertising:

- **Google Ads:** Runs pay-per-click (PPC) advertising campaigns automatically based on predefined rules and targets.
- **Facebook Ads Manager:** Provides ad scheduling, budget optimization, and audience targeting automation options.

9.Automation of Finance and Accounting:

- **QuickBooks:** This software automates accounting operations such as invoicing, expense monitoring, and financial reporting.

- **Xero:** A cloud-based accounting software that streamlines small business financial procedures.

10.Customer service and chatbots:

- **Zendesk:** Provides automated customer assistance via ticketing, knowledge base management, and chat connectivity.
- **Intercom:** Provides organizations with chatbot automation and client engagement capabilities.

11.Data Analytics and Reporting:

- **Google Analytics:** Automatically monitors website traffic, analyzes user behavior, and generates reports.
- **Intercom:** Tableau is a data visualization application for corporate intelligence that automates data analysis and reporting.

12.Automation of backup and security:

- **Back blaze:** Provides cloud backup and data storage solutions that are automated for data protection.
- **Norton:** Provides threat detection and protection cybersecurity automation technologies.

13.Automation in Human Resources and Recruitment:

- **Workday:** This software automates human resource procedures such as payroll, recruitment, and employee management
- **LinkedIn Talent Solutions:** Provides talent acquisition and job posting automation.

14.Automation of Inventory and Supply Chain:

- **SAP:** An ERP system that automates inventory management, supply chain management, and manufacturing operations.
- **Ship Station:** Order fulfillment and shipment automation for e-commerce firms.

These technologies and platforms can greatly increase your company's efficiency, minimize manual duties, and boost overall production.

Consider your specific business demands, integration capabilities, and scalability when picking automation technologies to ensure they correspond with your objectives and workflows. With the right automation solutions in place, you can concentrate on strategic initiatives and business growth while automating routine operations.

Creating efficient workflows

Workflow efficiency is the foundation of any successful firm. They assist you in increasing productivity, reducing errors, and completing jobs efficiently and on schedule. Whether you run a small business or a large organization, streamlining your workflows can result in major gains in your operations. Here's how to make effective workflows:

1. Define and Map Your Processes:

The first step in developing efficient workflows is identifying and documenting existing procedures. This entails dissecting each task or activity in a process and comprehending its purpose, dependencies, and inputs/outputs. Process mapping tools like as flowcharts and workflow diagrams can be quite useful for visualizing these processes.

2. Remove bottlenecks and redundancies:

After mapping out your processes, look for any superfluous stages or bottlenecks that are slowing down the workflow. Unnecessary approvals, double data entry, or human processes that can be automated are examples of redundancies. Bottlenecks are points in the process where work is delayed or stalled, usually owing to a lack of resources or inefficient procedures.

3. Automate Duplicate Tasks:

Automation is an extremely effective tool for streamlining procedures. Identify repetitive chores that can be automated with software or technologies. Email notifications, data entry, data validation, and document generation are all examples of this. Create rules and triggers in workflow automation software to automate certain operations based on predetermined conditions.

4. Streamline Processes:

Defining clear and consistent protocols that everyone in your organization can follow is what standardization entails. This minimizes errors and ensures that work is completed efficiently. Standard operating procedures (SOPs) should be documented and workers should be trained to ensure adherence.

5. Set Task Priorities and Deadlines:

Not all tasks in a workflow have the same level of priority or urgency. Set explicit timelines and prioritize tasks based on their impact on the overall process. To successfully track and manage deadlines, use project management tools or task management software.

6. Use Checklists and Templates:

Checklists and templates can help to simplify complex processes and reduce errors. They give personnel with a step-by-step roadmap to follow. You can make checklists for client onboarding, content production, and product launches, for example.

7. Simplify Communication:

Communication is essential for productive workflows. To facilitate communication among team members, use collaboration and communication technologies such as Slack, Microsoft Teams, or project management software. To avoid misconceptions, encourage clear and precise communication.

8. Performance Monitoring and Evaluation:

Monitor the performance of your workflows on a regular basis. Key performance indicators (KPIs) can assist you in determining how efficiently tasks are accomplished. Analyze data, solicit input, and pinpoint areas for improvement. Workflow management software, for example, can provide insights into workflow efficiency.

9. Constantly Improve:

Workflow improvement is a constant activity. Encourage an organizational culture of continual improvement. Encourage staff to make suggestions for improving workflows, and be willing to make adjustments based on feedback and data analysis.

10. Utilize Technology:

Integrate technology solutions that will help you with your workflows. Project management software, customer relationship management (CRM) systems, collaborative tools, and automation platforms are examples. Check that these tools are interoperable and work well together.

11. Adaptability and flexibility:

While standardization is crucial, workflows must also be adaptable to changing circumstances or unexpected events. Create contingency plans or alternative processes to deal with unexpected obstacles.

12.Employee Education and Engagement:

Invest in training and development to ensure that staff are knowledgeable about the procedures for which they are accountable. Employees should be included in the process improvement journey and encouraged to take ownership of their workflows.

Efficient workflows may boost your organization's productivity, cut costs, and increase customer happiness. You can stay flexible and competitive in today's dynamic business climate by constantly reviewing and optimizing your procedures. Remember that the goal is to perform activities not only faster, but also better, with fewer errors and higher efficacy.

Outsourcing and Delegation

Outsourcing and delegating are two critical techniques for companies that want to streamline their operations, focus on core capabilities, and scale effectively. These methods enable you to use external resources and disperse work, allowing your team to focus on high-impact activities. Let's look at the significance of outsourcing and delegation, as well as how to efficiently execute them.

Outsourcing:

1. Why Should You Outsource?

- **Cost effectiveness:** Outsourcing specific jobs or processes may be less expensive than recruiting full-time personnel. You can save money on salaries, benefits, and overhead.
- **Expertise:** Outsourcing gives you access to specialized experience and a pool of individuals with certain abilities, which might result in higher-quality results.
- **Focus on Core Functions:** Outsourcing non-core operations such as IT support, customer service, or accountancy frees up your internal team to focus on key responsibilities.
- **Scalability:** Depending on your business demands, outsourcing can allow you to quickly scale your operations up or down.
- **Global Talent:** You may access talent from all around the world to find the perfect fit for your specific needs.

2. Typical Outsourced Functions:

- **IT Services:** This category includes software development, cybersecurity, network management, and helpdesk support.
- **Customer Support:** Customer service, chat assistance, and call center operations can all be outsourced to boost customer satisfaction.
- **Accounting and finance:** Bookkeeping, payroll, and tax preparation are all services that can be outsourced.
- **Digital Marketing:** Commonly outsourced tasks include content production, SEO, social media management, and pay-per-click advertising.

- **Manufacturing and Production:** To cut expenses and focus on branding and marketing, some organizations outsource manufacturing or assembly processes.

3. How to Effectively Outsource:

- **Define Specific targets:** Determine what you want to achieve through outsourcing and set specific targets.
- **Select the Right Partner:** Choose the Right Outsourcing Partner: Research potential outsourcing partners, assess their expertise, and check references.
- **Clear communication:** Communicate your expectations, dates, and deliverables to your outsourcing partner in a clear and concise manner.
- **Monitor Progress:** Track the progress of outsourced jobs or projects on a regular basis and provide feedback as needed.
- **Protect Data:** When exchanging sensitive information with outsourced partners, ensure that data security and confidentiality are maintained.
- **Evaluate Performance:** Continuously analyze your outsourcing partner's performance to ensure they fulfill your expectations.

Delegation:

1. The Reason for Delegation:

- **Priorities:** Delegating work allows you to focus on high-priority obligations and strategic decision-making.
- **Skill Development:** Delegation provides opportunities for team members to learn new skills and take on more important roles.
- **Efficiency:** work distribution among team members can result in faster work completion and greater overall efficiency.
- **Empowerment:** Delegation empowers team members by assigning them specific tasks or projects, which can enhance morale and motivation.

2. How to Effectively Delegate:

- **Choose the Right jobs:** Determine which jobs can be delegated without jeopardizing quality or key outcomes.

Select the Right Person: Tasks should be assigned to team members depending on their skills, expertise, and workload.

- **Provide Specific Instructions:** Communicate the task's objectives, expectations, deadlines, and any resources required clearly.
- **Encourage Questions:** Encourage Team Members to Seek Clarification: Encourage team members to seek clarification and ask questions if they have any uncertainties.
- **Trust and Empower:** If possible, avoid micromanaging.
- **Track Progress:** Keep track of work progress, offer assistance as needed, and provide feedback once completed.
- **Recognize and Reward:** Recognize and thank: Thank and thank team members for their contributions and accomplishment of assigned duties.

Outsourcing and delegating can lead to increased productivity, cost savings, and a more focused and motivated staff. You may position your firm for development and success in today's competitive landscape by selecting the right jobs to outsource and empowering your staff through efficient delegation.

Chapter 7: Marketing and Promotion

Marketing and promotion are critical components of any thriving business. They allow you to engage with your target audience, raise brand awareness, and drive growth. In this chapter, we'll look at the fundamental components of efficient marketing and promotion methods that can help your company grow.

1. Recognize Your Target Audience:

Before you begin any marketing initiatives, you must have a thorough understanding of your target demographic. Who are your ideal clients? What are their wants, needs, and pain points? Conduct extensive market research to acquire insights and develop customer personas to drive your marketing tactics.

2: Developing Your Unique Value Proposition (UVP):

Your unique selling proposition (UVP) is what distinguishes your company from the competitors. It's a brief statement that emphasizes the distinct advantages and value your products or services provide to clients. Your unique value proposition (UVP) should be clear, compelling, and appealing to your target audience.

3. Establishing a Viable Online Presence:

A strong online presence is essential in today's digital world. Create and optimize your website, establish a presence on key social media networks, and consider launching a blog or podcast to contribute valuable material. Maintain consistency in your branding and messaging across all internet media.

4. Content Marketing

Content marketing is an effective method of attracting and engaging your target audience. Create high-quality, relevant content that speaks to the needs and interests of your target audience. This can include blog entries, videos, infographics, eBooks, and other forms of media. Consistent content development increases your industry's credibility and authority.

5. SEO (Search Engine Optimization):

Implement SEO tactics to increase the visibility of your website in search engine results. Improve your website's performance and mobile usability, and earn high-quality backlinks from trusted sources.

6. Email Promotion:

Email marketing is still a powerful tool for nurturing leads and engaging with your audience. Create a tailored and valued email list, create personalized and valuable email campaigns, and use automation to send targeted messages at the perfect moment.

7. Marketing on social media:

Choose social media networks that are relevant to your target demographic. To increase your reach, provide great material, interact with your fans, and use paid advertising. Social media can also be an effective avenue for customer service.

8.Pay-Per-Click (PPC) Marketing:

You can use PPC advertising to run adverts on search engines and social media platforms. Set clear goals, select the best keywords and audience targeting, and track ad performance to maximize ROI.

9.Influencer Marketing:

Collaboration with industry or specialized influencers can help you reach a larger audience and gain credibility. Choose influencers whose ideals are consistent with your business and products.

10. Analytics and Data-Driven Decision Making:

Track the effectiveness of your marketing activities with analytics tools. To make educated judgments and modify your plans, analyze website traffic, conversion rates, email open rates, and social media engagement.

11 Customer Comments & Testimonials:

To increase trust and credibility, display customer testimonials and reviews. Encourage happy consumers to tell others about their experiences, and consider developing a referral program.

12 Lifelong Learning and Adaptation:

The marketing landscape is constantly changing. Keep up to date on industry developments, emerging technology, and shifting consumer behavior. To remain competitive, you must be willing to change your marketing strategy.

13. Budget Administration:

Spend your marketing budget carefully. Keep track of the ROI for each marketing channel and change your budget allocation accordingly.

14. Ethics and Compliance:

Ensure that your marketing methods are in accordance with ethical standards and regulatory requirements. Respecting data privacy rules and being honest in your advertising are examples of this.

Marketing and promotion techniques that are effective are critical for expanding your organization and attaining long-term success. You can reach, engage, and convert customers while developing a strong brand presence in your sector by analyzing your audience, crafting a compelling UVP, and leveraging a mix of online and offline marketing channels. Remember that marketing is a continuous process that demands creativity, adaptation, and a strong dedication to providing value to your customers.

SEO And Content Marketing

SEO (Search Engine Optimization) and content marketing are two interconnected methods that play critical roles in driving organic traffic, improving search engine ranks, and increasing your company's online visibility. Let's take a closer look at each of these methods and see how they interact to form a successful digital marketing strategy.

1. Search Engine Optimization (SEO):

SEO is a comprehensive technique that aims to improve the visibility of your website and content in search engine results pages (SERPs). It entails a variety of approaches and best practices for making your website more search engine friendly.

This is how SEO works:

- **Keyword Research:** SEO begins with comprehensive keyword research to uncover the terms and phrases that your target audience is looking for. These keywords form the basis of your content strategy.
- **On-Page SEO:** On-page SEO is the process of optimizing individual web pages in order to increase their ranking. Meta titles, meta descriptions, header tags, and picture alt text are all important. It also requires strategically incorporating keywords into your text.
- **Technical SEO:** Technical SEO focuses on your website's technical elements, such as site speed, mobile friendliness. A well-optimized website improves user experience and is preferred by search engines.
- **Link Building:** Building high-quality backlinks from reliable websites is an important part of SEO. Backlinks act as "votes of confidence" in your content, informing search engines that it is valuable.
- **Content Quality:** SEO requires high-quality, useful, and relevant content. Websites that give valuable material to users are rewarded by search engines. Your material should respond to users' questions and meet their wants.
- **User Experience:** A great user experience, such as simple navigation, a clear site layout, and mobile friendliness, might have

an impact on your SEO rankings. Google, in particular, appreciates websites that put the user first.

- **Local SEO:** Local SEO is essential for businesses with physical locations. This includes optimizing your website for local searches, maintaining online reviews, and ensuring that your business information is correct across internet directories.

2. Content Promotion:

material marketing is a deliberate method to attracting and engaging a target audience that focuses on developing and delivering valuable, relevant, and consistent material. Blog posts, articles, videos, infographics, eBooks, podcasts, and other forms of content are all included in content marketing.

The following is how content marketing works:

- **Audience-Centric:** Content marketing starts with understanding your audience's demands, pain areas, and interests. Your material should offer solutions, answers, or entertainment to your target audience.
- **Content Creation:** Content marketers create a content calendar outlining themes, formats, and release dates. Based on keyword research and SEO best practices, high-quality content is developed.
- **Distribution:** Once material is developed, it must be efficiently promoted. This includes social media content sharing, email marketing, and outreach to industry influencers. The idea is to broaden your audience and increase traffic to your website.
- **Engagement:** It is critical to interact with your audience. Respond to comments, answer questions, and build a community around your work. Users who are engaged are more likely to become devoted consumers or followers.
- **Conversion:** The goal of content marketing is to lead users through the sales funnel. Not only should content enlighten and engage consumers, but it should also encourage them to do desired activities, such as signing up for newsletters, obtaining estimates, or completing purchases.

The Relationship Between SEO and Content Marketing:

SEO and content marketing are inextricably linked. Search engines look for substance and relevancy in content. When you create high-quality, useful material that corresponds to user search intent, you inadvertently add relevant keywords and phrases, which is an important component of SEO.

Effective content marketing can generate backlinks from other websites, increasing the authority and SEO rating of your site. Furthermore, by providing useful material on a regular basis, you keep your website fresh and encourage return visits from consumers, which might benefit SEO.

In contrast, SEO gives a foundation and direction for content marketing initiatives. SEO research assists content authors in determining which themes are popular and which keywords to target. Optimizing material for search engines guarantees that it may be found by users who are actively looking for information.

In essence, SEO and content marketing are two sides of the same coin that operate in tandem to increase your online presence and organic traffic. You can develop a strong online presence and attract and maintain your target audience by incorporating both tactics into your digital marketing plan and continuously publishing relevant, SEO-optimized content.

Social Media Strategies

Social media has become an essential component of modern marketing and communication, providing businesses with a powerful platform to connect with their target audience, raise brand awareness, and generate engagement. Creating good social media strategies is critical for using these channels to reach your business objectives. Here are the important steps to developing effective social media strategies:

1. Establish Specific Goals:

Begin by establishing clear, quantifiable, and time-bound objectives for your social media initiatives. Common goals include raising brand exposure, increasing website traffic, enhancing engagement, generating leads, and increasing sales.

2. Understand Your Audience:

Understand the demographics, interests, pain issues, and online behavior of your target audience. This insight informs your content development and allows you to personalize your messaging to your ideal customers.

3. Select the Appropriate Platforms:

Choose social media sites that are relevant to your audience and goals. Facebook, Instagram, Twitter, LinkedIn, Pinterest, and TikTok are all popular sites. Each platform appeals to a distinct audience as well as different content forms.

4.Create a Content Strategy:

Make a content calendar defining the types of content you'll post, the frequency with which you'll post, and the publishing times. Text postings, photos, videos, infographics, and tales should all be included. Maintain consistency in the voice and style of your brand.

5. Priority of Quality Over Quantity:

Concentrate on providing high-quality material that is valuable to your readers. Avoid content that is spammy or overly promotional. Engage your audience with postings that are useful, interesting, or inspiring.

6. Make Use of Visual Content:

Visual information, such as photographs and videos, is generally more engaging than text-only updates. Invest in generating eye-catching pictures that successfully express your message.

7. Make Use of User-Generated Content:

Encourage your fans to develop and share brand-related content. User-generated material lends authenticity and confidence to your message.

8. Communicate with Your Audience:

Respond to comments, messages, and mentions as soon as possible. Engage in meaningful conversations, respond to inquiries and concerns, and express gratitude for user involvement.

9. Make Use of Hashtags:

To increase the reach and visibility of your material, look for and apply relevant hashtags. To increase user engagement in campaigns and contests, create branded hashtags.

10.Paid Promotion:

Consider investing a chunk of your advertising budget to social media. Platforms provide a variety of targeting choices for reaching out to specific demographics and interests. Paid ads might help you expand and gain attention faster.

11. Examine and Adjust:

Analyze the performance of your social media initiatives on a regular basis using platform-specific metrics and third-party solutions. Keep track of important analytics like engagement rate, reach, clicks, conversions, and follower growth. Adapt your plan based on what works best for you.

12 Conduct Contests and Giveaways:

Organize competitions and freebies to encourage user participation and raise brand awareness. Check that the contest rules are consistent with the platform guidelines.

13. Partner and collaborate:

Use collaborations and partnerships with influencers, industry peers, or similar businesses to broaden your reach and tap into their current audiences.

14. Crisis Intervention:

Prepare for potential social media crises by developing a response strategy. Respond to unfavorable remarks or comments professionally and with empathy.

15. Stay Up to Date:

Keep up to current on social media trends, algorithm updates, and new platforms. Adapt your plan to be current and innovative.

16. Experiment and test:

Don't be afraid to experiment with different content forms, posting timings, or techniques. A/B testing can assist you in determining what is most appealing to your target audience.

17. Keep an eye on your competitors:

Monitor your competitors' social media strategies for insights and potential for difference.

It's important to remember that developing a successful social media presence takes time and regular effort. Your strategies should be consistent with your entire brand identity and business goals. You can effectively harness the power of social media to promote your brand and connect with your customers by constantly refining your strategy, remaining authentic, and stressing engagement and value to your audience.

Email Marketing Campaigns

Email marketing is still one of the most effective and cost-effective methods of engaging your audience, nurturing leads, and driving conversions. When done correctly, email marketing initiatives may generate strong returns on investment (ROI) and foster long-term consumer relationships. Here's a detailed guide on developing effective email marketing campaigns:

1. Establish Your Objectives:

Begin by defining your goals. What are your goals for your email marketing campaigns? Typical objectives include generating sales, building your subscriber list, increasing website traffic, and improving brand loyalty.

2. Create and Segment an Email List:

The cornerstone of your marketing is your email list. Sign-up forms on your website, social media, and other touchpoints can be used to collect email addresses. Segment your list based on parameters like demographics, buying history, or level of participation. Personalization is possible thanks to segmentation.

3. Select the Best Email Marketing Platform:

Choose an email marketing platform that meets your requirements. Mailchimp, Constant Contact, A Weber, and HubSpot are all popular solutions. These systems include list management, email design, automation, and analytics tools.

4. Create Interesting Content:

Create entertaining and valuable material that your audience will appreciate. Emails should be personalized with the recipient's name and content should be tailored to their interests and preferences. Newsletters, product updates, promotional offers, instructional resources, and event invitations are examples of common email content.

5. Create Emails That Are Mobile-Friendly:

Many people check their emails on their mobile devices. Make your emails mobile-responsive by using a responsive design that adapts to different screen sizes and orientations. Examine your emails on a variety of devices and email clients.

6. Create Captivating Subject Lines:

The subject line is the first thing people notice about your email. Make intriguing, succinct subject lines to attract recipients to open your emails. A/B testing can assist in determining which subject lines work the best.

7. Emphasis on Deliverability:

Avoid spamming behaviors that can jeopardize your email delivery. To confirm subscribers, use a double opt-in process, keep a clean list by eliminating inactive or bounced addresses, and adhere to email marketing best practices.

8.Personalization and segmentation are also important.

Use recipient names to personalize emails and recommend products or content based on previous interactions. Segmentation ensures that relevant material is delivered to each set of subscribers, enhancing engagement.

9. Test and Improve:

Test many aspects of your emails on a regular basis, including as content, design, call-to-action buttons, and sending times. To find opportunities for improvement, examine metrics such as open rates, click-through rates, conversion rates, and unsubscribe rates.

10. Campaign Automation:

Send personalized emails triggered by certain actions or events, such as welcome emails, abandoned cart reminders, or post-purchase follow-ups, using automation. Automation simplifies your work while also providing a personalized experience.

11. Analyze and monitor:

Utilize the tracking and reporting tools supplied by your email marketing platform to analyze email performance. Track crucial indicators to determine the performance of your marketing. Adjust your plan depending on data analysis results.

12. Comply with privacy laws:

Comply with data protection laws like the General Data Protection Regulation (GDPR) or the CAN-SPAM Act. Make sure you have clear permission from your subscribers to send them emails and provide opt-out options.

13. Interact and form relationships:

Encourage your subscribers to communicate with you in both directions. Include reply options in your emails and answer to requests or criticism as soon as possible. Developing true relationships with your target audience creates trust and loyalty.

14. Split Testing:

Conduct A/B tests on a regular basis to determine what works best for your audience. To optimize your email campaigns, experiment with alternative subject lines, content formats, graphics, and calls to action.

15. Continuous Improvement and Feedback:

Use surveys or direct correspondence to solicit feedback from subscribers. Use this input to improve your email marketing strategy and better cater to the requirements and preferences of your audience.

Email marketing campaigns can be an effective way to nurture leads, retain customers, and drive revenue. You can develop email campaigns that resonate with your audience and generate measurable results by concentrating on personalization, segmentation, valuable content, and continual improvement.

Paid Advertising Options

Paid advertising is an important part of any comprehensive marketing strategy. It enables you to reach a wider audience, attract traffic to your website, and swiftly produce leads or sales. several paid advertising methods are accessible across several platforms, each with its own set of advantages and targeting capabilities. Here's a rundown of some of the most popular paid advertising options:

1. Search Engine Promotion:

Google Ads: Formerly known as Google AdWords, Google Ads is one of the most popular pay-per-click (PPC) advertising systems. When people search for certain terms, it displays adverts at the top of Google's search results pages. Google Ads provides a variety of campaign types such as search ads, display ads, shopping ads, and video ads.

Bing Ads: Bing Ads, like Google Ads, allows you to design and run PPC ads on the Bing search engine and its network, which includes Yahoo. It can be an effective way to reach a different audience.

2.Social Media Marketing:

- **Facebook Ads:** Facebook provides a strong advertising platform with sophisticated targeting capabilities. You may develop highly targeted ads based on demographics, interests, and behaviors, and even retarget individuals who have previously interacted with your website or ads.
- **Instagram advertising:** Instagram advertising, which are part of Facebook's ad platform, allow you to reach a visually engaged audience. Instagram has a variety of commercial forms, such as photo ads, video ads, carousel ads, and narrative ads.
- **Twitter Ads:** To assist businesses in reaching their target audience, Twitter offers promoted tweets, promoted accounts, and promoted trends. Users might be targeted based on their interests, keywords, or demographics.
- **LinkedIn Ads:** LinkedIn is an excellent platform for B2B marketing. LinkedIn advertisements enable you to target professionals based on job title, company size, industry, and other criteria. There are choices for sponsored content, sponsored InMail, and display adverts.

3.Display Advertising:

- **Google Display Network:** The Display Network of Google reaches millions of websites, blogs, and apps. Text, graphics, and interactive media can all be used in display adverts. You can target specific websites, demographics, and hobbies, as well as remarket to visitors who have already visited your website.
- **Programmatic Advertising:** Programmatic advertising uses automated technologies to buy and position ads in real-time, optimizing ad delivery and targeting. It's commonly utilized for display and video advertisements on a variety of websites and apps.

4. Video Marketing:

- **YouTube advertising:** There are several video ad styles available on YouTube, including skippable advertising, non-skippable commercials, bumper ads, and display ads. Users' viewing habits and demographics can be used to target them.

5. Shopping Advertisements:

- **Google Shopping:** Google Shopping is ideal for e-commerce firms since it allows you to display product listings immediately in search results, replete with photographs, prices, and product specifications.

6.Novel Advertising:

- **Native Ads:** Native ads mix nicely with the platform's content, creating a less invasive and more engaging advertising experience. These advertisements are frequently seen on social media platforms, news websites, and content discovery tools.

7. Affiliate Promotion:

- **Affiliate Marketing:** Affiliate marketing, unlike traditional paid advertising, entails collaborating with affiliates who promote your products or services in exchange for a commission on sales earned by their efforts.

8. Remarketing and retargeting:

- **Remarketing/Retargeting:** This method entails displaying advertisements to users who have previously visited your website but did not convert. The goal of remarketing efforts is to re-engage these users and persuade them to take action.

9. Mobile Marketing:

- **Mobile Ads:** As mobile devices grow more popular, mobile advertising has become increasingly important. You may target customers on their smartphones and tablets by running mobile advertisements on search engines, social media platforms, and mobile apps.

10.Email Marketing:

- **Email Advertising:** Email marketing solutions allow you to run advertisements within email newsletters or send sponsored emails to a specific subscriber list.

11.Influencer Marketing:

- **Influencer Marketing:** Collaboration with influencers in your specialty or sector to promote your products or services to their engaged audience is an example of influencer marketing.

To optimize your return on investment (ROI) and fulfill your marketing objectives, a successful paid advertising campaign requires strategic planning, attentive monitoring, and continual optimization.

Chapter 8: Scaling Your Online Business

Scaling your online business is both an exciting and difficult stage of entrepreneurship. It entails growing your business, increasing revenue, and reaching a larger consumer base. This chapter examines critical techniques and factors for efficiently scaling your internet business:

1. Establish Specific Goals:

Define defined and quantifiable targets before going on a scaling adventure. These goals could include doubling your sales, expanding into new markets, introducing new product lines, or extending your consumer base. Clear objectives create focus and a sense of purpose.

2. Improve Operations:

Streamline your internal procedures and operations to better handle rising demand. Invest in technology, software, and automation techniques to cut down on manual labor and boost productivity. To meet rising demand, prioritize supply chain management, inventory control, and fulfillment operations.

3. Financial Preparation:

Ascertain that you have a good financial plan in place. As you scale, calculate your predicted costs, expected revenue, and possible profitability. Consider increasing your marketing budget, recruiting more employees, and growing your infrastructure. If necessary, secure appropriate funding.

4. Market Growth:

Investigate possibilities to broaden your market reach, both domestically and abroad. Conduct extensive market research to gain an understanding of local tastes, rules, and competitors. Customize your marketing and sales methods to appeal to a wide range of audiences.

5. Expand Your Product/Service Offerings:

Introduce new items or services that complement your current ones or target other client segments. Diversification can create new revenue streams and lessen reliance on a single product.

6. Spend money on marketing and advertising:

Set aside funds to boost your marketing efforts. Experiment with various advertising channels, such as paid advertising, content marketing, search engine optimization, and social media campaigns. Analyze ROI to determine which channels produce the best results and then invest accordingly.

7. Create a Scalable Technology Stack:

Invest in a scalable technological infrastructure capable of handling increased website traffic, transactions, and client interactions. Make sure your website can handle longer load times and remains responsive during peak hours.

8. Talent Acquisition and Hiring:

As your company expands, you may need to add to your workforce. Hire qualified people to assist you in managing various elements of your organization, such as marketing, customer service, operations, and finance. Create an organizational culture that attracts and keeps outstanding talent.

9. Retention of Customers:

While focusing on expansion, don't forget about your existing clients. Maintain solid client relationships by providing exceptional service, offering loyalty programs, and communicating in a personalized manner. Customers that are pleased with your services are likely to become your most outspoken supporters.

10.Data-Informed Decision-Making:

Make informed judgments by leveraging data analytics. Monitor key performance indicators (KPIs), watch consumer behavior, and use data-driven insights to improve your plans and uncover possibilities for growth.

11 Scalable Customer Service:

Invest in customer support technologies that can manage additional questions while maintaining a consistent experience. To streamline support operations, consider chatbots, self-service portals, and customer relationship management (CRM) solutions.

12.Maintaining Quality:

As you grow, keep your focus on providing high-quality products or services. Quality is vital for long-term success and customer pleasure. Avoid sacrificing quality in the name of expansion.

13.Legal and Compliance:

Ensure that your company complies with all applicable laws and regulations in your target areas. If you plan to develop abroad, seek legal guidance to help you manage international legislation.

14. Iterate and monitor:

During the scaling phase, continuous monitoring and adjustments are required. Prepare to make changes in response to market input, shifting customer preferences, and changing industry trends.

15. Risk Control:

Determine potential scaling risks, such as increased competition, market changes, or operational issues. Create risk-mitigation techniques to address these threats ahead of time.

Scaling your online business is a difficult but rewarding task. While it is not without its difficulties, careful planning, smart execution, and a commitment to providing value to your consumers will help you achieve sustainable growth and propel your firm to new heights.

Growth Strategies and Tactics

Growth is a key goal for all businesses. Growth plans and methods are critical for success, whether you're a startup hoping to get traction or an established organization looking to expand further. Here's a thorough guide on accelerating business growth:

1. Market Expansion:

- **Tactic:** Increase your market share inside your current market.
- **Strategy:** Increase sales of current items or services to existing customers or explore new customer categories. This can include aggressive marketing, discounted pricing, loyalty programs, and improved customer service.

2.Expansion of the Market:

- **Tactic:** Enter new markets or geographical locations as a tactic.
- **Strategy:** Research and find markets where your offerings are in high demand. Adapt your products, marketing, and distribution tactics to the new market's demands and tastes.

3. Product Creation:

- **Tactic:** Create and market new items or services as a tactic.
- **Strategy:** Innovate by creating new items that meet client wants or improve on existing ones. Before investing in development, conduct market research to uncover opportunities and validate demand.

4.Diversification:

- **Tactic:** Expand into new product or service categories as a tactic.
- **Strategy:** Expand into similar or unrelated markets to mitigate risk and provide new revenue streams. To mitigate probable issues, conduct adequate research and planning.

5. Acquisition and merger (M&A):

- **Tactic:** Acquire or merge with other companies as a strategy.

- **Strategy:** Mergers and acquisitions can help you acquire access to new markets, technologies, and customer bases. To ensure a smooth merger process, identify relevant firms and conduct due diligence.

6. Strategic Partnerships and Alliances:

- **Tactic:** Form alliances with other businesses as a strategy
- **Strategy:** Form alliances with complementary enterprises to capitalize on each other's capabilities. Strategic relationships can result in shared resources, greater reach, and new customer access.

7. Franchisee:

- **Tactic:** Expand your business concept by franchising it.
- **Strategy:** Franchising enables people to copy your company under your brand and leadership. It's an efficient approach to expand quickly while sharing risks and rewards with franchisees.

8. E-commerce and online presence:

- **Tactic:** Establish a strong internet presence as a tactic.
- **Strategy:** Increase online sales by leveraging digital marketing, SEO, social media, and e-commerce platforms. Pay attention to user experience and mobile optimization.

9.Customer Retention and Upselling:

- **Tactic:** Retain existing clients and encourage larger spending as a tactic.
- **Strategy:** Customer relationships should be nurtured through great service, individualized communication, and loyalty programs. Offer comparable products or premium services to cross-sell and upsell.

10. Data-Informed Decisions:

- **Tactic:** Use data analytics to gain strategic insights.
- **Strategy:** Make informed decisions by analyzing customer data, market trends, and key performance indicators (KPIs). Data-driven

insights can be used to direct marketing initiatives, product enhancements, and budget allocation.

11 Employee Development and Training:

- **Tactic:** Invest on staff skills and expertise as a tactic.
- **Strategy:** A well-trained workforce can promote innovation, improve customer service, and increase productivity. Provide continuing training, mentorship initiatives, and opportunities for career advancement.

12 Cost Reduction:

- **Tactic:** Identify cost-cutting opportunities.
- **Strategy:** Review and optimize your operational expenses on a regular basis. This could entail renegotiating contracts, using more efficient technology, or reevaluating your supply chain.

13. Customer Evaluation and Improvement:

- **Tactic:** Gather and act on customer feedback as a tactic.
- **Strategy:** Customer input is crucial for improving products and services. To find areas for improvement and solve client pain points, use surveys, reviews, and direct encounters.

14.Branding and Reputation Management:

- **Tactic:** Strengthen your brand's identity.
- **Strategy:** A strong brand may command greater prices as well as increased consumer loyalty. To develop a positive reputation in your sector, invest in branding, narrative, and public relations.

15.Scalable Technology:

- **Tactic:** Invest in scalable technology solutions as a strategy.
- **Strategy:** Ensure that your IT infrastructure can support future development. Scalable systems, cloud computing, and automation can help you grow without disrupting your operations.

16. International Growth:

- **Tactic:** Exploration of global markets is a tactic.
- **Strategy:** International expansion can help you diversify your customer base. When going worldwide, consider concerns such as localization, compliance, and market entry tactics.

17. Constant Innovation:

- **Tactic:** Foster an innovative culture as a tactic.
- **Strategy:** Encourage your organization's inventiveness and experimentation. Innovation can result in new products, better processes, and a competitive advantage.

Successful growth initiatives include meticulous planning, flexibility, and a dedication to providing value to your customers. Choose methods and strategies that are in line with your company's goals and market conditions, and be prepared to change your approach as your company grows. Remember that sustainable growth is a journey, not a destination, and that it necessitates a long-term outlook.

Expanding Product Offerings

Extending your product options is a smart step that can boost business growth and competitive advantage. Here's how to successfully increase your product offers, whether you're a startup looking to diversify or an established corporation searching for additional cash streams:

1. Market Analysis:

- **Understand Customer wants:** Begin by researching your target market and learning about their wants, preferences, and problem areas. This knowledge will assist you in identifying product gaps that can be filled with new offerings.
- **Analyze Competitors:** Research your competitors to see what products or services they provide that you do not. Examine their product offerings and client satisfaction to determine their strengths and weaknesses.

2. Product Portfolio Evaluation:

- **Current Product Evaluation:** Evaluate the performance of your current products or services. Determine which are thriving and which are underperforming or nearing the end of their lives.
- **Identify Synergies:** Look for natural synergies between your current goods and prospective future items. Consider how new items can complement or improve on your current ones.

3. Customer Reaction:

- **Seek Input:** Interact with your customers to learn about their wants and requirements. Customer feedback can help you personalize new product offers to their preferences and efficiently solve trouble issues.
- **Beta Testing:** Consider launching pilot or beta versions of new products to a restricted set of clients for testing and feedback if possible. This helps you to fine-tune your offerings before launching them on a large scale.

4. Research and Innovation:

- **R&D Investment:** Set aside funds for research and development (R&D). Invest in innovation to develop one-of-a-kind, high-quality items that stand out in the marketplace.
- **Stay Informed:** Keep up to current on industry developments, developing technology, and changing client demands. Attend trade exhibitions, conferences, and industry events to learn and be inspired.

5. Product Creation:

- **Prototyping and Testing:** Create prototypes and put them through rigorous testing to confirm your new goods' usefulness, durability, and quality. Before mass production, resolve any concerns.
- **Cost Analysis:** Determine the expenses of product development, manufacturing, and marketing. Check to see if new products are financially viable and fit inside your budget.

6.Segmentation of the Market:

- **Determine Target Segments**: Determine which client segments will benefit the most from your new offerings. To effectively reach these categories, tailor you're marketing and sales techniques.
- **Personalization:** Tailor your marketing communications to each target segment's individual demands and interests.

7. Logistics and distribution:

- **Inventory Management:** Make plans for your inventory and supply chain logistics in order to handle the new products. Make sure you can meet demand without overstocking or understocking.
- **Distribution Channels:** Determine whether your current distribution channels are capable of handling the delivery of new products. If necessary, look into new distribution channels or collaborations.

8. Promotion and Marketing:

- **Launch Plan:** Create a complete marketing and promotion strategy for your new products. To raise awareness and enthusiasm, consider teaser campaigns, product releases, and continuous marketing initiatives.

- **Leverage Existing Customer Base:** Introduce the new products to your existing customer base. Give loyal consumers access to exclusive previews or exclusive deals.

9. Education and Training:

- **Internal Training:** Ensure that your sales and customer support workers are well-versed in the new goods. They should be able to efficiently respond to client inquiries.
- **Customer Education:** Provide materials such as product guides, videos, and FAQs to educate customers about the new products' features and benefits.

10. Iteration and Feedback:

- **Collect Feedback:** Gather feedback from customers and internal teams on the performance and reception of new products on an ongoing basis. Use this input to make changes and improvements.
- **Iterate and innovate**: Be open to modifying your product offerings in response to market input and evolving client wants. Long-term success is dependent on the ability to adapt.

11 Monitoring and Measuring:

- **Key performance indicators (KPIs):** Establish key performance indicators (KPIs) to track the success of your product growth activities. To evaluate performance, track sales statistics, customer satisfaction, and profitability.
- **Adjust Strategies:** Adjust your strategies if specific products aren't functioning as intended. This could include adjusting marketing strategies, pricing, or product features.

Extending your product options is a dynamic and gratifying process that involves careful preparation, market insight, and a dedication to providing value to your consumers. You may successfully diversify your product portfolio and generate business growth if you follow these tactics and remain responsive to market input.

Entering new markets

Expanding into new markets is an important step for any company aiming to expand its reach and revenue. Entering new markets involves careful strategy and execution, whether you're a startup wanting to explore unexplored potential or an established company looking to diversify. Here's a detailed strategy to successfully expanding into new markets:

1. Market Analysis and Research:

- **discover Potential Markets:** To begin, discover potential markets that correspond with your business objectives. Consider population size, economic stability, purchasing power, and cultural significance.
- **Assess Market Demand:** Determine the market demand for your products or services. To understand client wants and preferences, conduct extensive market research, including surveys, focus groups, and competitor analysis.
- **Regulatory and Legal Considerations:** Research the new market's legal and regulatory needs. Trade rules, intellectual property laws, and industry-specific requirements may all have an impact on your operations.

2. Strategy for Market Entry:

- **Market Segmentation:** Market segmentation is the process of dividing a target market into categories based on demographics, psychographics, and purchasing behavior. Determine the most promising segments to concentrate your efforts.
- **Entry Mode:** Select the best entry mode for your company. Exporting, licensing, franchising, joint ventures, acquisitions, and forming a wholly-owned subsidiary are all options. Choose the mode that best fits your resources and market dynamics.

3. Product and Service Customization:

- **Product Localization:** Product localization is tailoring your products or services to the demands and preferences of the target market. This could include changes to features, packaging, pricing, or even rebranding.

- **Cultural Sensitivity:** Keep cultural variances in consideration while marketing, branding, and advertising.

4 Budget for Market Entry:

- **Financial Planning:** Create a budget that includes market research, legal fees, marketing and advertising charges, and operational setup. To avoid financial burden, plan for contingencies.
- **Financial predictions:** Develop financial predictions including revenue expectations and anticipated expenses for the first few years in the new market.

5. Local Collaborations and Alliances:

- **Local Partners:** Consider creating alliances or collaborations with local businesses or distributors. Local partners can give vital insights, network access, and on-the-ground assistance.
- **Distribution Channels:** Determine which distribution channels are most effective for your products or services. This could include wholesalers, merchants, e-commerce platforms, or direct sales, depending on the market.

6.Marketing and branding:

- **Market Entry Strategy:** Create a detailed market entry strategy including your marketing approach. Adapt your marketing strategy to local market circumstances and consumer behavior.
- **Digital Presence:** Create a strong online presence by creating a localized website, social media accounts, and search engine optimization (SEO) tactics targeted to the target market.

7. Regulatory Adherence:

- **Legal Compliance:** Ensure that all local rules and regulations are followed, including permits, licenses, taxes, and product certifications. Seek legal guidance to help you negotiate the complexities of regulatory environments.

8. Operational Configuration:

- **Local Infrastructure:** Establish the physical infrastructure required by your business model, such as offices, warehouses, or manufacturing facilities.
- **Supply Chain Management:** Optimize your supply chain to efficiently fulfill local demand. This could entail locating local suppliers or developing effective logistics.

9. Human Capital:

- **Talent Acquisition:** Hire local personnel who are knowledgeable about the market and culture. Invest in training and development to create a staff that is both talented and culturally aware.
- **Cultural Sensitivity:** Develop a business culture that honors and respects local customs, traditions, and values. Cultural awareness is essential for establishing relationships and trust in a new market.

10.On-going monitoring and adaptation:

- **KPI Tracking:** Establish key performance indicators (KPIs) to track the development of your market entry. Assess sales, consumer input, and market developments on a regular basis to make educated modifications.
- **Adaptation:** Be prepared to modify your strategies in response to market feedback and changing conditions. Flexibility and agility are critical when entering new markets.

Entering new markets is a dynamic and hard venture, but it may lead to corporate growth and success with comprehensive research, strategic planning, and a commitment to knowing and satisfying local client needs. You can confidently extend your firm into new markets by following these tactics and remaining sensitive to market trends.

Collaborations and Partnerships

Partnerships and collaborations have become essential strategies for firms to grow and achieve mutual success in today's interconnected business landscape. These joint ventures enable organizations to capitalize on each other's strengths, share resources, and seize new opportunities. Here's an in-depth look at the relevance of partnerships and collaborations, as well as tactics for developing them:

The Importance of Collaborations and Partnerships:

1. **Shared Expertise:** Collaborations bring together the pooled knowledge and expertise of multiple organizations. This collaboration has the potential to result in creative solutions and a better grasp of industry trends.
2. **Sharing Resources:** Companies can pool their resources, such as funds, technology, and talent, to pursue common goals more efficiently and cost-effectively.
3. **Risk Mitigation:** Organizations can better overcome obstacles and uncertainties by sharing responsibility.
4. **Market Expansion:** By collaborating with other organizations, you can gain access to new markets, consumer groups, or geographical regions that would otherwise be impossible to enter on your own.
5. **Market Expansion:** Partnerships with renowned organizations can boost your brand's credibility and reliability among customers and stakeholders.
6. **Innovation Acceleration:** Collaboration typically develops an innovative culture, enabling the sharing of ideas and the development of ground-breaking goods or services.

How to Form Successful Partnerships and Collaborations:

1. **Find Complementary Partners:** Look for partners whose skills and experience complement your own. Take into account what each firm can offer to the table in order to develop a synergy that benefits both sides.
2. **Set Clear Objectives and Expectations:** Define the partnership's aims and objectives from the start. To achieve alignment, outline each organization's duties, expectations, and contributions.

3. **Set Mutually Beneficial Terms:** Agree on terms that are fair and equitable to both parties. Revenue-sharing schemes, profit-sharing arrangements, and intellectual property rights are all examples of this.
4. **Develop Trust and Communication:** Encourage open and transparent communication among all parties involved. Maintain open lines of communication and provide regular updates to build trust in your partnership.
5. **Legal Agreements & Contracts:** Collaborate with legal experts to design thorough agreements that safeguard all parties' interests. Contracts should include crucial provisions such as dispute resolution, termination clauses, and confidentiality.
6. **Cultural Alignment:** Determine the cultural compatibility of companies. A unified set of values and principles can have a substantial impact on the collaboration's success.
7. **Continuous Evaluation and Improvement:** Evaluate the partnership's development and performance on a regular basis. Identify areas for improvement and make the required changes to improve the efficacy of the partnership.

Partnerships and Collaborations Come in a Variety of Forms:

1. **Strategic Alliances:** Strategic alliances are formed by businesses to pursue common goals such as cooperative product development, market expansion, or research activities.
2. **Joint Ventures:** A joint venture is formed when two or more organizations form a separate legal company to carry out a specific project or business venture. Each participant often has a stake in the business.
3. **Cross-Promotions and Marketing Collaborations:** Businesses join forces to market and promote their products or services, using each other's client bases and distribution networks.
4. **Supply Chain Collaborations:** Companies work together to optimize their supply chains, cut costs, and improve efficiency in the manufacturing and distribution of commodities.
5. **Partnerships in technological:** Organizations collaborate to develop or integrate technological solutions that improve their goods or services.
6. **Collaborations in Research and Development:** Companies join forces to conduct research and development activities, typically combining resources to innovate and tackle challenging problems.

7. **Collaborations for Nonprofit and Social Impact:** Organizations work together on social or environmental initiatives to effect positive change in society or to address global concerns.

Partnerships and collaborations that are successful involve devotion, communication, and a shared commitment to attaining common goals. Businesses may generate growth, innovation, and long-term success while building mutually beneficial connections within their sectors and communities by deliberately forming and cultivating these partnerships.

Chapter 9: Managing Finances and Taxes

Finance and tax management are key components of running a successful business. This chapter examines critical techniques and factors for maintaining great financial health and ensuring tax compliance.

1. Budgeting and Financial Planning:

- **Make a Comprehensive Budget:** Create a complete budget that accounts for all revenue, expenses, and projected costs. To keep on track, examine and alter your budget on a regular basis.
- **Cash Flow Management:** Keep a close eye on your cash flow to ensure you have enough liquidity to handle operational needs, investments, and unexpected emergencies.

2.Accounting and record-keeping:

- **Maintaining Accurate and Organized Financial Records:** Keep accurate and organized financial records. To ensure precision and compliance, use accounting software or hire a professional accountant.
- **Regular Reconciliation:** Reconcile bank statements, invoices, and accounts on a regular basis to discover and address discrepancies.

3. Financial Reports:

- Prepare regular income statements (profit and loss statements) to track your revenue, expenses, and net income. These statements provide information on the financial success of your company.
- **Balance Sheet:** A balance sheet is used to keep track of your assets, liabilities, and equity. A balance sheet provides a snapshot of your company's financial status at a given point in time.

4. Tax Preparation:

- **Tax Liability Analysis:** Understand your local, state, and federal tax requirements. Analyze tax rules and regulations to legally reduce your tax liability.
- **Tax Calendar:** Keep track of tax dates and filing procedures. Failure to meet deadlines may result in penalties and interest costs.

5. Expense Control:

- **Cost Control:** Evaluate your spending on a regular basis and discover areas where cost-cutting or optimization is achievable. Improve profitability by implementing cost-cutting methods.
- Negotiate with suppliers and vendors to obtain better price, discounts, or favorable payment conditions.

6. Debt Administration:

- **Debt Assessment:** Evaluate your company's debt and its influence on cash flow. Make a plan for managing and reducing your debt over time.
- Examine your possibilities for refinancing or consolidating high-interest debts in order to minimize your overall interest costs.

7. Financial Analysis and Reporting:

- **Financial Ratios:** Calculate and evaluate key financial ratios such as liquidity ratios, profitability ratios, and solvency ratios to gain insight into the financial health of your company.
- **Monitoring Key Performance Indicators (KPIs):** Track key performance indicators (KPIs) related to your industry to assess the effectiveness of your financial initiatives.

8. Growth and Investment Strategies:

- **Capital Allocation:** Decide how to allocate capital for expansion, investments, and reserves. Determine the probable return on investment for different projects and efforts.
- **Risk Assessment:** Assess the risks associated with financial decisions and devise mitigation solutions.

9.Tax Compliance:

- **Maintain Exact documents:** Keep careful documents to support your tax filings. Organize invoices, receipts, payroll records, and other financial paperwork.

- Working with tax professionals or advisors that specialize in small business taxation is a good idea. They can assist with ensuring compliance and identifying tax-saving options.

10. Financial Software and Tools:

- Accounting software, budgeting tools, and financial management platforms can all be used to streamline financial procedures and increase accuracy.

11 Emergency Reserve Fund:

- Create an emergency fund to meet unanticipated expenses or revenue deficits. This provides financial security during difficult times.

12. Payroll Taxes and Employee Benefits:

- Maintain compliance with payroll tax rules, including as income tax withholding, Social Security, and Medicare contributions.
- **Employee Benefits:** To recruit and retain talent, consider providing employee benefits like as retirement plans, health insurance, and other incentives.

Effective financial management and tax compliance are critical for your company's long-term viability and success. You may handle the complexity of finances and taxes while developing a financially healthy and resilient firm by adopting strong financial habits, remaining informed about tax regulations, and getting professional help when necessary.

Financial tracking and budgeting

Financial tracking and budgeting are important habits for both people and corporations. They lay out a clear path for managing income and expenses, making informed financial decisions, and working toward long-term financial goals. In this section, we'll discuss the significance of financial tracking and budgeting, as well as critical success tactics.

The Value of Financial Monitoring and Budgeting:

- **Clarity and Awareness:** Financial tracking is keeping track of all income and expenses. It provides a thorough view of your financial condition, assisting you in understanding where your money comes from and goes.
- Budgeting extends this by establishing financial goals and allocating resources accordingly. It gives an organized framework for achieving your financial goals.
- **Financial Control:** Financial tracking and budgeting allow you to take control of your finances. You can uncover opportunities for improvement by tracking your spending patterns and comparing them to your budget.
- **Emergency Planning:** Creating an emergency reserve is an important element of budgeting. It guarantees that you have funds set aside to handle unforeseen expenses such as medical bills, car repairs, or job loss.
- **Debt Management:** By keeping track of your financial data, you can examine your debt condition. Budgeting allows you to arrange funds to pay off existing debt and prevent accruing new debt.
- Budgets are useful tools for attaining financial goals, such as saving for a vacation, purchasing a home, or planning for retirement. They provide a road map for allocating resources to achieve these goals.
- **Peace of Mind**: Knowing that you have financial control and a strategy in place helps minimize financial stress and worry. It gives you peace of mind and improves your entire well-being.

Effective Financial Tracking and Budgeting Strategies:

Keep a record of every transaction:

- Track every source of income and expense, no matter how minor. To make the process easier, use apps, spreadsheets, or budgeting tools.
- Expenses should be organized into categories such as housing, transportation, groceries, entertainment, and savings. This classification assists in identifying places where you can reduce back or reallocate expenditures.

Set specific objectives:

- Establish defined, measurable financial objectives. Having specific objectives inspires budget adherence, whether it's paying off credit card debt, saving for a down purchase, or building an emergency fund.
- **Make a Realistic Budget:** Create a budget that matches your income, expenses, and financial objectives. Ascertain that it is both achievable and long-term sustainable.
- **Track on a regular basis:** Update your financial records on a regular basis and compare actual costs to your budget. This continuous monitoring allows you to make changes as needed.
- **Automate Savings:** As soon as you receive income, set up automatic transfers to your savings or investing accounts. This "pay yourself first" strategy guarantees constant savings.
- Build an emergency fund that will cover at least three to six months of living expenses. If necessary, start small and progressively build the fund over time.
- **Review and Adjust:** Review your budget and financial goals on a regular basis. Life conditions vary, and your budget should adapt to keep up.
- **Seek Professional Help:** If you're feeling overwhelmed or dealing with complicated financial issues, consider seeing a financial advisor or planner. They can provide tailored advice and recommendations.
- **Maintain Discipline:** Discipline is essential for good budgeting and financial tracking. Stay away from impulsive purchases and stick to your budget.

Financial tracking and budgeting are not about limiting your spending, but rather about making deliberate decisions that match with your financial goals. These behaviors, when followed regularly, can help you attain financial stability, reduce stress, and strive toward a secure financial future.

Tax considerations for online businesses

Online firms, like their brick-and-mortar counterparts, must deal with a variety of tax duties and considerations. Understanding these tax effects is critical for ensuring compliance and streamlining financial operations. Here's an in-depth look at tax implications for online businesses:

1. Organizational Structure:

- **lone Proprietorship:** As a lone proprietor, your business income is usually reported on your personal tax return. On your profits, you must pay income tax and self-employment tax.
- **LLC, Corporation, or Partnership:** Your tax liabilities and filing requirements may differ depending on the business form you choose. Consult a tax expert to discover the most tax-effective structure for your internet business.

2.Sales Tax:

- **Considerations for the Nexus:** Determine whether you have a sales tax nexus in each state. Nexus is a large presence that necessitates the collection and remittance of sales tax on transactions in those states.
- Sales tax automation software can assist you handle sales tax collection and reporting. This can aid in the simplification of compliance across multiple countries.

3.Income Tax:

- Self-employed persons and business owners may be required to make quarterly anticipated tax payments to satisfy income and self-employment tax responsibilities.
- **Deductions and Credits:** Learn about the tax breaks and credits available to internet businesses. Deductions for home office expenses, business-related travel, and technology investments are examples of these.

4.E-commerce Platforms:

- Many e-commerce systems include sales and transaction data that can help with tax reporting. Check that the reporting features on your platform are accurate and dependable.
- **1099-K Forms:** If you use third-party payment processors such as PayPal or Stripe, be aware that they may send 1099-K forms to report your income to the IRS. Check to see if the stated income matches what you have on file.

5. International Business:

- **VAT/GST:** If you sell to overseas customers, be aware of your country's Value Added Tax (VAT) or Goods and Services Tax (GST) duties. Registration, collection, and remittance of these taxes may be required for compliance.
- **Currency Conversion:** When dealing with overseas sales, be mindful of currency conversion rates and their impact on your financial records and tax calculations.

6. Taxes on Employees and Contractors:

- **Payroll taxes:** If you have employees, you must withhold income taxes, Social Security taxes, and Medicare taxes from their pay.
- **Independent Contractors:** To avoid misclassification charges, properly categorize workers as employees or independent contractors. Independent contractors must pay their own taxes.

7. Keeping Records:

- **Keep Exact Records:** Maintain meticulous records of income, expenses, receipts, and financial activities. These documents are required for tax compliance and audits.
- Digital receipts and invoices are used by many internet businesses. Ensure that these documents are well-organized and securely preserved so that they can be easily retrieved.

8. Tax Preparers:

- **Seek Expert Advice:** Consider consulting with a certified tax specialist, such as a CPA or tax counselor who specializes in small businesses or internet commerce. They can provide specialized advice and assist you in maximizing deductions.

9 Local and State Taxes:

- Local Business Taxes or Licensing costs: Some localities levy local business taxes or licensing costs. Check with your local government to ensure that you are in compliance.
- Property taxes may be applicable if you have actual goods or property in a specific location.

10.Tax Compliance Software:

- **Tax Software:** Invest in trustworthy tax compliance software or services to aid you in accurately computing and filing your taxes. For smooth tax management, many platforms interface with e-commerce systems.

11 Year-End Preparation:

- **Tax Preparation**: As the year comes to a close, go over your financials and speak with a tax professional about year-end tax planning techniques. Deductions, contributions to retirement accounts, and income deferral are all examples of this.

Online firms must keep up to date on changing tax legislation and be proactive in meeting their tax obligations. Consult with tax professionals on a regular basis, keep correct records, and use technology to make tax compliance easier. By approaching taxes strategically, internet businesses can reduce obligations, optimize financial operations, and focus on development and innovation.

Legal Compliance and Business Structure

Legal compliance and selecting the correct business structure are critical aspects when beginning or running a firm, and they can have a substantial impact on your operations, liabilities, and financial responsibilities. Let's look at these critical elements and their significance in developing a successful firm.

Legal Obligation:

Legal compliance is critical for protecting your company from any legal troubles, fines, and reputational damage.

Consider the following essential aspects of legal compliance:

1. Commercial Licenses and Permits:

- Determine the specific licenses and permits needed for your business at the federal, state, and municipal levels. General business licenses, health permits, and industry-specific licenses are examples of these.
- **Application and Renewal:** Submit the appropriate applications and renewals in order to receive and keep the essential licenses and permissions.

2. Registration and Tax Identification Numbers:

- **Legal form:** Determine the best legal form for your company (e.g., sole proprietorship, LLC, corporation) and register it with the proper authorities.
- **Employer Identification Number (EIN):** If your company employs workers or operates as a corporation or partnership, you must obtain an EIN from the Internal Revenue Service (IRS).

3. Labor and Employment Laws:

- **Employee Classification:** To comply with labor laws and tax requirements, properly identify workers as employees or independent contractors.
- **Wage and Hour Laws:** Comply with federal and state minimum wage, overtime, and other labor rules.

4. Tax Obligation:

- **Income Taxes:** Understand and comply with your federal, state, and local income tax requirements. This includes tax returns as well as expected tax payments.
- **Sales Tax:** Collect and remit sales tax in line with state and municipal legislation, if applicable. Determine whether your company has a sales tax nexus in specific areas.

5. Intellectual Property Rights:

- **Trademarks and Copyrights:** When necessary, protect your intellectual property by registering trademarks or copyrights. This protects your brand's identification as well as your creative works.
- **Trade Secrets:** Take precautions to safeguard your company's confidential information and trade secrets.

6. Agreements and Contracts:

- **Written Agreements:** Use well-drafted contracts to document commercial ties, partnerships, and transactions. Contracts can aid in the avoidance of disputes and the clarification of expectations.
- **Contractual Obligations:** Make certain that you and your business partners follow the terms and conditions of contracts and agreements.

7. Data Security and Privacy:

Data Protection Laws: Comply with all applicable data privacy laws and regulations. Protect consumer and staff data to avoid data breaches.

8. Environmental Requirements:

- **Environmental Compliance:** If your business activities have an influence on the environment, follow environmental standards and get any permissions or approvals that are required.

9.Selecting the Best Business Structure:

- Choosing the right business structure is a vital decision that impacts your company's responsibility, taxes, and governance.

Consider the following typical business structures:

1.Sole Proprietorship:

- The advantages are simplicity, complete control, and direct tax reporting.
- Personal liability, limited access to funds, and probable difficulty in raising capital are all disadvantages.

2. LLC (Limited Liability Company):

- Benefits include limited personal liability, adaptable management, and pass-through taxation.
- Cons: Some cases are complicated, and there are fewer choices for equity funding.

3. Business:

- Benefits include limited personal liability, a separate legal organization, and access to equity financing.
- Cons include complicated administrative requirements, double taxation for C businesses, and more formal governance.

4.Collaboration:

- Advantages include shared management and profitability, pass-through taxation, and access to a wide range of expertise.
- Personal liability, probable disagreements, and collaborative decision-making are all disadvantages.

5. Charitable Organization:

- Benefits include tax-exempt status for eligible uses as well as eligibility for grants and donations.
- **Cons:** Profit distribution is limited, and nonprofit requirements must be strictly followed.

6. Collaborative:

- Pros include shared ownership and decision-making, equal profit sharing, and an emphasis on the community.
- **Cons:** Complex governance and the possibility of conflict.

7.Seek Professional Help:

- Navigating legal compliance and selecting the best business structure can be difficult. It is best to seek the advice of legal and financial experts who specialize in business law and taxation. They can provide tailored advice based on your company's specific needs and objectives.

You establish a firm foundation for your business's success and longevity by prioritizing legal compliance and selecting the most appropriate business structure. Compliance not only protects your company, but it also fosters trust among customers, partners, and investors, resulting in a great reputation in the marketplace.

Chapter 10: Avoiding Common Pitfalls and Challenges

Running a successful online business is a gratifying experience, but it is not without its obstacles and hazards. In this chapter, we'll look at some of the most typical challenges that internet businesses confront and offer solutions for avoiding or surmounting them.

1. Insufficient Market Research:

- **Pitfall:** Inadequate market research can result in the release of a product or service that does not fulfill the needs or wants of customers.
- **Solution:** Make thorough market research a priority in order to understand your target audience, competition, and market trends. To remain relevant, keep your research up to date on a regular basis.

2. Inadequate Business Planning:

- **Pitfall:** Failure to have a strong business plan can lead to aimless operations and financial insecurity.
- **Solution:** Create a detailed business plan outlining your objectives, strategy, financial estimates, and contingency measures. As your company grows, revisit and revise your strategy.

3. Financial Overstretch:

- **Pitfall:** Excessive spending or taking on too much debt might put a burden on the financial sustainability of your organization.
- **Solution:** Use rigorous financial management, create a budget, and keep careful tabs on expenses. Make substantial financial commitments only if there is a clear return on investment.

4. Failure to Meet Legal and Tax Obligations:

- **Pitfall:** Failure to comply with legal and tax duties can result in penalties, lawsuits, and reputational harm.

- **Solution:** Stay up to date on legal and tax obligations, seek professional advice as necessary, and prioritize compliance. Maintain thorough records and adhere to deadlines.

5. Ineffective Marketing Techniques:

- **Pitfall:** Ineffective marketing can lead to limited awareness, fewer leads, and slow growth.
- **Solution:** Continuously improve your marketing techniques, test new channels, and invest in analytics to track performance. Concentrate on developing a strong internet presence.

6.Ignoring Customer Feedback:

- **Pitfall:** Ignoring client feedback can stymie product development and harm your brand's reputation.
- **Solution:** Seek and value client input actively. It can be used to improve your products, services, and customer experience.

7. Excessive Scaling:

- **Pitfall:** Scaling your business too quickly can strain resources and lead to operational inefficiencies.
- **Solution:** Prioritize regulated, long-term growth. Make sure your company can handle rising demand without sacrificing quality.

8. Insufficient Cybersecurity:

- **Pitfall:** Failure to implement cybersecurity measures can lead to data breaches, loss of customer trust, and legal consequences.
- **Solution:** Invest in strong cybersecurity procedures such as encryption, regular software updates, and employee security training.

9 Inadequate Time Management:

- **Pitfall:** Poor time management can result in burnout, missed opportunities, and lower production.
- **Solution:** Establish good time management practices, establish priorities, delegate chores if possible, and minimize multitasking.

10. Failure to Recognize Trends and Innovation:

- **Habit:** Stagnation and neglecting industry trends might render your company obsolete and less competitive.
- **Action:** Keep up with industry developments, new technologies, and client preferences. Accept innovation as a means of adapting and evolving.

11.Failure to Adapt to Market Changes:

- **Fallacy:** Inflexibility and reluctance to change might expose your company to market shifts and disruptions.
  Solution: Promote an adaptability and agility culture. Be open to pivoting and adjusting methods as needed.

12 Ignoring Work-Life Balance

- **Habit:** Overworking and disregarding personal well-being can result in burnout and reduced creativity.
- **Solution:** Set limits, prioritize work-life balance, and schedule time for relaxation and self-care.

Resilience, adaptability, and a commitment to constant development are required for online business success. You may manage problems with confidence and develop a robust and profitable online business by recognizing and proactively resolving these frequent hazards. Keep in mind that failures are opportunities for growth, and that tenacity is essential for long-term success.

Overcoming burnout and motivation dips

Burnout and low motivation are significant obstacles that many people, especially internet business entrepreneurs, face on their entrepreneurial journey. However, with the appropriate tactics and mindset, you can overcome these challenges and rekindle your passion and productivity. In this section, we'll look at how to recover from burnout and rediscover your motivation:

Identifying Burnout:

- **Recognize the Signs:** Everyone's burnout develops differently, but common symptoms include persistent weariness, decreased productivity, cynicism, and a lack of enthusiasm in your work. Recognizing these signs is the first step toward recovery from burnout.
- **Examine the Causes:** Consider the things that have contributed to your burnout. Excessive workload, unrealistic expectations, personal life difficulties, or a lack of work-life balance could all be factors.

Burnout Resilience Techniques:

- **Self-Care and Well-Being:** Make self-care a priority by getting adequate sleep, eating healthily, and engaging in regular physical activity.
- To deal with stress and anxiety, try mindfulness, meditation, or relaxation techniques.
- **Set Boundaries:** Make clear distinctions between work and personal life. Make a separate workplace for yourself and arrange regular breaks to refresh.
- **Delegate and Seek Help:** Don't be afraid to delegate or outsource duties or responsibilities that are causing you stress.
- Seek the advice of mentors, business peers, or a therapist to discuss problems and obtain new views.
- Time Management: To increase productivity and avoid burnout, use time management strategies such as the Pomodoro technique or time blocking.

Getting Back on Track:

- **Reconnect with Your Why:** Think about why you started your internet business in the first place. Reconnecting with your passion and purpose can help you rediscover your motivation.
- **Set precise, Achievable Goals:** Define precise, attainable goals for your organization. To create a sensation of accomplishment, break things down into smaller, manageable tasks.
- **Celebrate tiny Victories:** Recognize and celebrate your accomplishments, no matter how tiny. This type of positive reinforcement can increase motivation.
- Seek inspiration and learning from successful businesses, books, podcasts, or industry events. Learning from others can help you rediscover your passion.
- **variation and Innovation:** To avoid boredom, include variation into your regular routine. To stay involved, try out new strategies, goods, or services.
- **Collaboration and networking:** Make contact with others in your sector or community who share your interests. Project collaboration and networking can bring new perspectives and drive.

Keeping Long-Term Motivation:

- **Develop a progress Mindset:** View obstacles and failures as chances for progress. A growth mindset promotes resilience and long-term motivation.
- **Reevaluate and Adjust on a Regular Basis:** Reevaluate and adjust your business goals and tactics on a regular basis. Be willing to change and evolve in response to changing conditions.
- **Find Joy in the Process:** Instead of focusing simply on outcomes, shift your attention to finding joy and fulfillment in the daily process of establishing and expanding your business.
- **Seek Passion Projects:** Look for side projects or efforts that connect with your interests and passions. These can breathe new life into your work.
- **Accountability and Support:** Participate in mastermind groups or accountability partnerships to hold yourself accountable for your progress and stay motivated.

Remember that fatigue and low motivation are common occurrences, particularly for entrepreneurs. The goal is to handle them proactively and devise tactics to keep your health and excitement for your internet business intact. You may overcome burnout and reignite your enthusiasm to achieve long-term success by prioritizing self-care, creating clear goals, and keeping connected to your passion.

Dealing with Market Changes and Competition

In the fast-paced world of internet commerce, responding to market changes and remaining competitive are critical for long-term success. Markets change, consumer preferences fluctuate, and new competitors emerge, so entrepreneurs must have strategies in place to overcome these obstacles. Key considerations and strategies for dealing with market changes and competition are as follows:

1. Ongoing Market Monitoring:

- **Keep Up to Date:** Monitor industry news, trends, and market reports on a regular basis. This allows you to predict changes in client behavior and new opportunities.
- **Customer input:** Pay attention to your customers' input and make changes to your products or services as needed. Their perspectives can be really beneficial.

2. Competitive Evaluation:

- **Understand Your Competition:** Research your competitors' plans, strengths, and shortcomings. Identify market gaps that you can exploit or areas in which you can differentiate yourself.
- **Benchmarking:** Compare your company to industry leaders on a regular basis to uncover opportunities for improvement.

3. Change and Innovation:

- When market conditions change, be ready to pivot and adjust swiftly. This may necessitate changes to your product offers, marketing methods, or business model.
- Invest in research and development to stay ahead of the competition and innovate. Determine how you can provide distinct value to your customers.

4. Experimentation:

- **Product and Service Portfolio:** Diversify your product and service offerings to appeal to a larger consumer base or to different market niches.

- **Revenue Streams:** To lessen dependency on a single income source, investigate different revenue streams such as subscriptions, one-time sales, affiliate marketing, or digital products.

5. Customer-First Approach:

- Prioritize client satisfaction and cultivate good relationships. A happy consumer is more likely to return and refer others.
- **Personalization:** When possible, tailor your offers and marketing messaging to particular customer preferences.

6. Branding and marketing:

- Invest in a strong and memorable brand that speaks to your target audience. A well-known brand can help you stand out from the crowd.
- **Digital Marketing:** To effectively reach and engage your audience, use digital marketing tactics such as content marketing, SEO, social media advertising, and email marketing.

7. Acquisition and Retention of Customers:

- Implement successful customer acquisition techniques to broaden your reach and acquire new customers.
- **Customer Retention:** Put equal focus on customer retention. Repeat business from happy clients might be less expensive than gaining new ones.

8. Flexibility:

- **Infrastructure:** Create a scalable infrastructure capable of handling rising demand. Scalability is critical for expansion without losing quality.

9. Strategic Alliances:

- **Collaborations:** Look into strategic alliances with complementary businesses to broaden your reach and gain access to new client segments.

10.Management of Risk:

- **Planning for Emergencies:** Create a plan for mitigating potential risks and interruptions. Be ready for unanticipated market fluctuations or economic downturns.

11. Customer Feedback:

- **Data Analytics:** Use data analytics and customer insights to make educated judgments and adapt your tactics to changing customer behaviors.

12.Patience and perseverance:

- **Long-Term Outlook:** Maintain a long-term perspective and recognize that success often necessitates perseverance in the face of obstacles and disappointments.

The process of adapting to market changes and competition is ongoing. Vigilance, creativity, customer-centricity, and strategic planning are all required. Your internet business may not only weather market shifts but also thrive in an ever-changing landscape if you keep aware, nimble, and nurture an innovative culture. Remember that adaptability and resilience are essential for long-term success.

Keeping Current with Industry Trends

Staying current with industry trends is not only an option in the fast-paced world of online company; it is a requirement. Keeping an eye on your industry's pulse allows you to make informed decisions, identify emerging possibilities, and stay competitive. Here's how you keep up with industry developments effectively:

1. Lifelong Learning:

- **Read Industry Publications:** Sign up for industry magazines, journals, and blogs. These publications frequently include the most recent trends, research, and perspectives.
- Enroll in online courses or webinars relevant to your industry. These can provide extensive knowledge as well as practical skills.
- **Podcasts and Webinars:** Subscribe to industry podcasts and attend webinars where experts discuss current trends and share their experiences.

2. Participate in Industry Events:

- **Conferences and Trade fairs:** Attend industry-related conferences and trade fairs in person or remotely. These events offer networking possibilities as well as direct knowledge about developing trends.
- **Networking:** Attend these events to meet peers, industry leaders, and professionals. Share your knowledge, exchange ideas, and cultivate useful contacts.

3. Participate in Professional Organizations:

- Consider joining industry-specific professional organizations. These organizations frequently provide materials, bulletins, and events to keep members up to date.
- **Forums and Discussions:** Take part in relevant online forums or discussion groups. Conversations with peers might bring immediate insights.

4. Make use of social media:

- **Follow Influential Figures:** On sites such as Twitter and LinkedIn, follow industry influencers, experts, and thought leaders. They frequently share useful information and articles.
- **Join Industry Organizations:** Participate in LinkedIn groups or Facebook communities connected to your industry. Discussions and knowledge sharing are facilitated by these groups.

5. Keep an eye on news and press releases:

- Set up Google Alerts for keywords relevant to your sector. You will be notified when new articles or news pieces are published.
- Keep an eye out for press releases from prominent players in your business. They frequently announce new goods, projects, or strategic alliances.

6. Competitive Evaluation:

- Monitor your competitors' websites, social media profiles, and marketing materials on a regular basis. This can disclose their most recent products and strategy.
- **SWOT study:** Conduct a SWOT (Strengths, Weaknesses, Opportunities, and Threats) study to uncover trends that may have an impact on your firm.

7.Reports and studies from the industry:

- **Market Research studies:** Access market research studies tailored to specific industries. These frequently feature extensive data as well as insights about current and future trends.
- **Academic Studies:** Search for academic studies and research articles in your subject. They can provide in-depth knowledge of new trends.

8. Experiment and be creative:

- **Pilot Projects:** Experiment with new trends or technology in your business on a small scale. This hands-on experience can assist you in determining their potential impact.
- Establish teams or individuals inside your firm that are responsible for researching and adopting creative trends.

9. Maintain Your Inquisitiveness:

- Instill a culture of inquiry in your team by asking questions. Encourage team members to inquire about industry trends and seek answers.
- **Feedback Loops:** Establish feedback loops with customers and clients in order to better understand their changing needs and preferences.

10.Strategic Planning:

- **Incorporate Trends:** Consider incorporating important industry trends into your strategic planning process. Consider how these trends might affect the future of your company.

Keeping up with industry changes is a continuous endeavor that necessitates dedication and an open mind. Accept the problem as a chance for growth and innovation. You'll position your online business for long-term success in a dynamic and competitive economy by remaining informed and adjusting to changing environments.

Chapter 11: Case Studies of Successful Online Entrepreneurs

In this chapter, we'll look at the inspiring stories of great online entrepreneurs who have navigated the digital terrain, battled hurdles, and achieved extraordinary success. Their experiences offer vital insights and lessons that can inspire and educate prospective online entrepreneurs. Here are some noteworthy case studies:

Case Study 1: Jeff Bezos of Amazon

It has grown into the world's largest online retailer, offering a diverse range of items and services.

Important Takeaways:

- Bezos emphasized the significance of consumer happiness and convenience, which inspired innovations such as Amazon Prime and same-day delivery.
- **Long-Term Vision:** Amazon has lost money for years while focusing on growth and market dominance. Bezos kept a long-term outlook and invested in technology and infrastructure.
- Amazon has diversified its business beyond e-commerce to include cloud computing (Amazon Web Services), entertainment (Amazon Prime Video), and hardware (Kindle and Echo devices).

Case Study 2: Brian Chesky, Nathan Blecharczyk, and Joe Gebbia of Airbnb

Background: In 2008, three friends decided to rent out air mattresses in their flat during a conference because motels were scarce. Since then, it has evolved into a global hospitality platform.

Important Takeaways:

- Airbnb challenged the traditional hotel industry by providing novel and economical housing options. They used technology to build a peer-to-peer marketplace.

- **Adaptation:** In different markets, Airbnb experienced regulatory and legal problems. They were able to adapt by collaborating with local governments and addressing safety concerns.
- **Community Building:** Airbnb concentrated on developing trust and loyalty among its user base by fostering a feeling of community among hosts and guests.

Case Study 3: Tobi Latke, Daniel Weinand, and Scott Lake of Shopify

- Tobi Latke and his co-founders founded Shopify in 2006 to provide businesses with e-commerce solutions. It has evolved into a leading e-commerce platform, with millions of entrepreneurs using it.

Important Takeaways:

- **Empowering Entrepreneurs:** Shopify's purpose is to improve commerce for all. They offer tools and information to help businesses prosper online.
- **Scalability:** Because Shopify's platform is highly scalable, businesses can start small and grow into enormous organizations without switching e-commerce platforms.
- Shopify is constantly adapting to market developments and trends, such as the advent of drop shipping and the significance of mobile shopping.
- Case Study 4: Eren Bali, Gagan Biyani, and Oktay Caglar of Udemy
- Udemy was established in 2010 as an online learning platform. It enables anyone to create and sell courses on a variety of subjects.

Important Takeaways:

- **Education Access:** Udemy democratized education by offering a platform for instructors all over the world to share their knowledge and for learners to access low-cost courses.
- **Global Reach:** Udemy's reach extends to over 190 countries, breaking down educational geographical restrictions.
- Udemy's founders believe in the potential of continual learning and flexibility, which matches with the platform's objective.

These case studies demonstrate the variety of successful online enterprises as well as the numerous roads to success. These entrepreneurs have exhibited resilience and devotion to their objectives through customer-centricity, innovation, adaptation, or empowerment. Aspiring internet entrepreneurs can learn from their experiences and get inspiration as they launch on their own business adventures.

Inspiring stories of individuals success

Financial success is frequently the result of years of hard work, persistence, and steadfast dedication to one's goals. These inspiring stories of people who have achieved financial success against all odds show that anything is achievable with the correct mindset and determination.

1. Elon Musk, Visionary Entrepreneur:

- Elon Musk, the CEO of Tesla and SpaceX, is well-known for his lofty ambitions in space exploration and sustainable transportation.
- **Inspiration:** Musk's vision and determination have resulted in ground-breaking breakthroughs ranging from electric vehicles to reusable rockets, transforming industries and accumulating a fortune.

2. Oprah Winfrey, Media Entrepreneur and Philanthropist:

- Oprah Winfrey, a media star, survived a difficult childhood to become a famous talk show host, media owner, and philanthropist.
- **Inspiration:** Winfrey's commitment to personal development, media empire, and charity initiatives demonstrates the transformational power of self-belief and tenacity.

3. The Sage of Omaha, Warren Buffett:

- **Background:** Warren Buffett is regarded as one of the world's most successful investors, owing to his disciplined value investing philosophy.
- Buffett's consistent investing style, long-term vision, and devotion to continuing learning have made him a millionaire and an investment icon.

4. J.K. Rowling - From Robbery to Robbery:

- J.K. Rowling, the creator of the Harry Potter series, overcame various obstacles before becoming one of the world's wealthiest authors.

- **Inspiration:** Rowling's story emphasizes the value of perseverance in the face of rejection and adversity, which eventually leads to literary success and financial independence.

5. Mark Zuckerberg, social media Pioneer:

- **Background:** While still in college, Mark Zuckerberg co-founded Facebook, the world's largest social networking site.
- **Inspiration:** At a young age, Zuckerberg's entrepreneurial energy, imaginative thinking, and passion to connecting people around the world catapulted him to financial success.

6.Starbucks' Transformation: Howard Schultz

- Howard Schultz established Starbucks as a global coffeehouse franchise and brand powerhouse.
- **Inspiration:** Schultz's unwavering pursuit of a vision, emphasis on the customer experience, and social consciousness led to Starbucks' extraordinary success and his own financial fortune.

7. Steve Jobs, Apple's Visionary:

- Steve Jobs co-founded Apple Inc. and pioneered personal computing, music, and cellphones.
- **Insight:** Jobs' drive to product perfection, design aesthetics, and persistent commitment to innovation helped him become a legendary character and helped Apple become one of the world's most valuable corporations.

8.The Virgin Empire Builder: Richard Branson

- **Background:** Richard Branson founded the Virgin Group, a conglomerate that includes music, aviation, telecommunications, and other businesses.

These inspiring examples show that financial success can be achieved via a combination of vision, hard work, resilience, and creativity. While everyone's route to success is different, they all share characteristics like determination, adaptability, and the guts to pursue their objectives. These stories serve as reminders that no matter where one begins in life, financial success is within grasp with determination and steadfast belief in one's goals.

Key takeaways from their journeys

Elon Musk, Oprah Winfrey, Warren Buffett, J.K. Rowling, Mark Zuckerberg, Howard Schultz, Steve Jobs, and Richard Branson's paths give several essential.

lessons that should inspire and assist anyone seeking for financial success:

1. **Vision and Persistence:** These people had a clear vision of what they wanted to achieve and were persistent in pursuing it, even in the face of adversity. Their unrelenting dedication to their vision demonstrates the value of perseverance in achieving financial success.
2. **Resilience and Overcoming Adversity:** Many of these successful people encountered considerable hurdles and setbacks along the way. Their experiences emphasize the significance of resilience and the ability to overcome failures and hurdles.
3. **Innovation and Creativity:** Innovation and creativity were critical to these persons' success. They were always looking for innovative ways to solve problems, disrupt industries, and give distinctive solutions that people could relate to.
4. **Continuous Learning:** These individuals shared a dedication to personal improvement and lifelong learning. They were open to new ideas, welcomed change, and were constantly eager to learn and grow.
5. **Taking Calculated Risks:** Financial success frequently necessitates the taking of calculated risks. While hardly reckless, these individuals were willing to leave their comfort zones and make deliberate moves that could result in huge rewards.
6. **Passion and Purpose:** Each of these people was completely committed to their work and felt a strong sense of purpose. Their enthusiasm fueled their effort and kept them motivated even during difficult moments.
7. **Adaptability:** Their success was dependent on their ability to adapt to shifting conditions and market dynamics. They were adaptable and willing to change course when necessary to remain relevant and competitive.
8. **Customer Focus:** Many of them stressed the necessity of knowing and addressing the demands of their customers. Putting the client

at the heart of their enterprises resulted in high customer loyalty and long-term success.

9. **Long-Term Perspective:** These people frequently have a long-term perspective, realizing that financial achievement could take time. They were willing to make short-term investments and sacrifices for long-term advantages.
10. **Giving Back:** Several of these rich people have become well-known philanthropists, highlighting the value of giving back to society after achieving financial success. Their charitable contributions have benefited a variety of causes and localities.
11. **Building Strong Teams:** They understood the importance of forming strong teams and surrounding themselves with brilliant people who complemented their skills. Their success was dependent on effective leadership and teamwork.
12. Despite their accomplishments, many of these people remained humble and grounded. They knew that their success was due not only to their own efforts, but also to the contributions of people around them.

While everyone's journey is different, these fundamental principles can help anyone who wants to be financially successful. These lessons emphasize the significance of determination, adaptability, invention, and a dedication to lifelong learning on the route to financial prosperity, whether in business, investing, writing, or any other sector.

Conclusion

To summarize, the concept of an online passive income business is definitely tempting in the digital age, providing individuals and entrepreneurs with a practical approach to accelerate the financial success of their online business. Individuals can use their time, skills, and expertise to develop various streams of income that can generate revenue around the clock, even while they sleep, using this strategy.

Affiliate marketing and drop shipping are two examples of online passive income enterprises, as are blogging, e-books, and digital courses. They enable people to diversify their income sources, lessen their financial reliance on a single employment or traditional firm, and attain more financial stability.

Building a successful online passive income business, on the other hand, is not a get-rich-quick plan. Setting up the essential infrastructure and creating valuable content or products requires dedication, hard work, and a large initial investment. Furthermore, continual maintenance and optimization are required to ensure that the business continues to provide passive income.

Furthermore, online passive income businesses, like any other company initiative, are fraught with problems and risks. In many niches, competition is severe, and market dynamics can shift quickly. Long-term success requires adapting to changing trends and remaining current with the latest digital marketing methods.

Finally, an online passive income business can be an important part of a larger financial strategy. It provides the possibility of financial independence, flexibility, and the ability to make money while pursuing other interests or spending time with loved ones. However, realistic expectations, a desire to invest time and effort, and a commitment to staying informed and adaptive in the ever-changing digital ecosystem are all required. An online passive income business can be a strong instrument for speeding financial success in the online world if approached with the appropriate mindset and a good strategy.

www.ingramcontent.com/pod-product-compliance
Lightning Source LLC
Chambersburg PA
CBHW082337270726
48658CB00017B/2876
9798874031473